THE
PENNSYLVANIA RAILROAD
A PICTORIAL HISTORY

BOOKS BY E. P. ALEXANDER · THE PENNSYLVANIA RAILROAD:
A PICTORIAL HISTORY · IRON HORSES · MODEL RAILROADS

THE PENNSYLVANIA RAILROAD

A PICTORIAL HISTORY

BY EDWIN P. ALEXANDER

BONANZA BOOKS • NEW YORK

TO
ALBERTA

CONTENTS

PREFACE

Now THAT the Pennsylvania Railroad has passed its hundredth anniversary, the time is particularly appropriate for noting the more important events of its growth and progress. The contents of this book constitute a summary of its history, rather than a full account—which would take volumes. Coupled with the many rare and hitherto unpublished reproductions of old prints and other pictorial matter, it presents a story of how the Pennsylvania Railroad grew into the world's greatest transportation system.

Since the Pennsylvania continues to develop, its history cannot be complete; therefore somewhat more attention is given herein to its inception and early growth, most of the latter having taken place during its first thirty years (today, except for the acquisition of the Long Island Railroad and holdings in some Eastern roads, it serves essentially the same territory as it did in the seventies). Important too, are the System's contributions to railroading in general. Many of today's "standards"— such as the air brake—were first tried and used on its lines, and their importance is not to be overlooked.

Often graphic comparison between early and modern locomotives, rolling stock, track, stations, bridges, and other features shows the continual progress and development better than a written description. Therefore the illustrative material constitutes the major part of this sketch of the Pennsylvania Railroad, without which it would never have been attempted. With the exception of some contemporary photos furnished by courtesy of the railroad, nearly all the illustrations have come from the author's collection.

For the valuable assistance I have had in locating research material and general information pertaining to the Pennsylvania Railroad, I particularly wish to acknowledge the co-operation of Mr. Walter Pertuch, Librarian of the Franklin Institute, Mr. Paul T. Warner of the Baldwin

Locomotive Works, and Miss E. M. Ferguson, Librarian of the Pennsylvania Railroad. Mr. Howard Gilbert of the Pennsylvania Publicity Department, Mr. A. O. Geertz, Fuel Engineer, Pennsylvania Railroad, and Mr. Thomas Hanna of the *Mutual Magazine* have also kindly assisted in furnishing data. My sincere thanks to them and others whom I have had occasion to call upon.

PART ONE

THE ORIGIN AND DEVELOPMENT OF THE PENNSYLVANIA RAILROAD

THE STORY of the Pennsylvania Railroad begins, not with the date of its charter, but more than a score of years earlier.

Of all the pioneers of railroading, the first and most important was undoubtedly Colonel John Stevens. To him on February 6, 1815, was granted the first charter for a railroad in America—for a railroad between New Brunswick and Trenton—approximately where the Pennsylvania's New York Division is today. But in Stevens' own words, ". . . the public mind was not sufficiently enlightened to induce moneyed men to embark their funds in a project then considered wild and impracticable."

On March 13, 1823, a charter was granted Stevens by the Pennsylvania State Legislature authorizing the construction of a railroad from Philadelphia to Columbia. Even at that time Stevens planned its extension westward, for he remarked, "And when this great improvement in transportation shall have been extended to Pittsburgh, then thence into the heart of the extensive and fertile State of Ohio, and also the great western lakes, Philadelphia may then become the grand emporium of the western country. . . . The improvement, when once introduced, will unquestionably be extended from Philadelphia across New Jersey to the City of New York." Although early surveys for the line were made at Stevens' expense, lack of sufficient funds and opposition by politicians who favored canals prevented any actual construction. Few people, too, at that time believed that steam locomotion was practical, so perhaps it was only natural that in 1824 the Pennsylvania State Legislature appointed a board of canal commissioners who were to report on the feasibility of a water route to the west.

Then in 1825 came the opening of the Erie Canal across New York. Almost immediately the bulk of western trade was attracted through this route, and as a result Philadelphia began to lose her prestige in trade. Although previously the Quaker City had been the financial and industrial center of the country, New York now became *the* metropolis. It soon became apparent to Philadelphians that an improved means of travel across Pennsylvania to the Ohio River was imperative if any trade was to be retained. So in 1826 an act was passed by the legislature providing for the start of the "Pennsylvania Canal"; and on July 4, ground was broken near Harrisburg.

During this same year the Columbia, Lancaster and Philadelphia Railroad Company was incorporated, the act repealing the Stevens charter but covering substantially the same route proposed in 1823. The following year the state legislature, seeing that the private enterprise made no headway, directed the Canal Commissioners to lay out and contract for the construction of a railroad over this route and also to report on the possibility of a line from Huntington to Johnstown. An appropriation of $2,000,000 was made for this work and for the canal system already started. Major John Wilson located the Columbia Railroad in 1827, reporting favorably for such a line rather than a canal between Philadelphia and the Susquehanna River owing to lack of water. On March 24, 1828, the legislature passed an act authorizing the construction of the railroad, the principal difference between this and early proposals being that it had now become a state enterprise.

Twenty miles at each end of the line was to be started at once and $2,000,000 was set aside for this work. In April 1828 the surveys were begun by Major Wilson, and by December 6 he reported them completed. Construction was contracted for in April 1829, work was immediately started, and before the end of the following December, forty miles of grading, viaducts, and bridges were finished. To facilitate construction, parts of the line were put into use with horse-drawn cars as soon as completed, and by September 20, 1832, the line from Philadelphia to Paoli was in full service. Later in the fall of the same year, an excursion train with the Norris locomotive "Green Hawk" left the head of the Belmont Inclined Plane and ran to Paoli and back, taking nine hours for the trip.

On October 7, 1834, the line was officially opened. Two trains drawn by the Baldwin locomotives "Lancaster" and "Columbia" left Columbia at 8 A.M. carrying Governor Wolf, the Canal Commissioners, state officials, engineers, and guests, arriving in Philadelphia at 6 P.M. Until 1836, however, horses were generally used. These were supplied largely by the state, while the various types of cars were privately owned, a fixed toll being charged for their transport. In 1836, locomotives superseded horsepower, some seventeen being reported that year.

The Philadelphia and Columbia Railroad was interesting in its physical aspects in that inclined planes were used at each end of its line. From the west end of the Columbia Bridge across the Schuylkill River in Philadelphia, the Belmont Plane rose 1 foot in 15 for a distance of 2805 feet—a total rise of 187 feet. A 60-horsepower stationary engine supplied the power for operating a 9-inch rope to which the cars were attached and pulled up or let down the plane. A similar arrangement was installed at the Columbia end of the line on the Susquehanna River, where the plane was 1800 feet long with a rise of 1 in 20—the total rise being 90 feet. Risks and delays were frequent at the Belmont Plane, as this account of a very early accident shows:

We learn from the news books of Mr. Potts, that as one of the cars attached to the "People's Line," on the Columbia Road, was yesterday morning descending the inclined plane, the bolt which prevents the wheels from running, came out of the break, when the car descended with such rapidity and violence, that it was dashed to pieces. The agent, Mr. Beatty, a young man, was holding the break on the car, when he was violently thrown under, and mangled in so shocking a manner, that no hopes can be entertained of his recovery. He was taken up insensible, and carried to the Third Street hall, where he now remains.

Fortunately the passengers had got out of the car, before it began to descend, and walked down, thereby preventing a much more melancholy occurrence.[1]

Because of these physical difficulties and a high operating cost of $27,000 yearly, other routes for entering Philadelphia were planned soon after it was put into use. One of the first was the West Philadelphia Railroad Company, incorporated in 1835, which left the main line at what is now Ardmore and reached the Schuylkill just south of Market Street. Because of financial difficulties it was later taken over by the Canal Commissioners and finished by them, and on October 14, 1850, trains began using this line, whereupon the Belmont Plane was abandoned. The so-called Permanent Bridge at Market Street was strengthened in 1850 to carry two tracks, and in 1852 the passenger depot at 18th and Market Streets was opened. Bingham and Dock, leasing the eastern line from the State, operated it with and for the Pennsylvania Railroad until 1857, when the latter purchased it.

The second stage of travel west to Pittsburgh was on the Middle Division Canal of the State System, which, from the terminus of the railroad at Columbia, followed the east bank of the Susquehanna River to Middletown, where it joined the river. Crossing at Duncan's Island, it entered the valley of the Juniata, which it followed to Hollidaysburg. Its length of 172 miles contained 33 aqueducts, and the total height overcome was 585.8 feet, by means of 111 locks.

At Hollidaysburg transfer was made to the Allegheny Portage Railroad, a remarkable feat of engineering for the early days of rail transportation. Approved by the State Legislature on March 21, 1831, construction was begun the following month, and the road was completed and opened for traffic November 26, 1834. A second track was laid down

[1] Hazard's *Register of Pennsylvania,* June 1835.

two years later. From Hollidaysburg a series of five inclined planes in a distance of ten miles carried the line to the summit at Blair's Gap, a rise of 1398 feet. On the western side of the Allegheny Mountains the rise was 1172 feet from Johnstown in 20 miles, in which five planes were also built. On the comparatively level stretches between planes, horses were first used, and later locomotives. There were 153 culverts and 4 viaducts, including the Conemaugh Viaduct and the 900-foot Staple Bend Tunnel, first in America.

Two 30-horsepower engines were installed at the top of each inclined plane, and one at a time was used to drive the rope to which trains (without locomotives) were attached. The first ropes were 7½ inches in diameter; these, because they slipped from their grooves in the guide wheels, were later replaced with 8-inch ropes. In 1842 some of the first wire cables made by Roebling's were put into use. Traffic was so worked that an ascending train and a descending train were always attached to the rope at the same time, as it served the two parallel tracks. Several devices for braking were employed, the upper wheel having a power-operated brake, and a so-called "buck" car was usually hitched behind the train. The time for moving a train up or down was about five minutes; the cars could be attached to the rope in two and a half minutes and 24 cars could be passed up (and the same number down) in an hour. During the six months ending October 31, 1836, 19,171 passengers and 37,081 tons of freight were transported in 14,300 carloads. The water supply for the stationary engines was a source of continual trouble and expense, having sometimes to be brought more than a mile through wooden pipes.

From Johnstown, the final stage traveling westward to Pittsburgh was by the Western Division Canal, which extended some 104 miles following the valleys of the Conemaugh, Kiskiminetas, and Allegheny rivers. It had 152 bridges and 16 aqueducts, and a 1,000-foot tunnel and 66 locks overcame a height of about 465 feet. Because of occasional low water, a dam across a branch of the Conemaugh was built to remedy this deficiency—the same dam whose failure years later was to cause the Johnstown flood.

As early as 1836 the Canal Commissioners were directed to find a route which would eliminate the use of the inclined planes, but the usual procrastination evident in most matters pertaining to the State System prevented any action until 1851. This was several years after the Pennsylvania Railroad had started construction of its line, and finally in 1855 the new railroad, costing the state $2,143,355, was put into service under the name of New Portage Railroad.

Despite the service they performed, these State Works were far from satisfactory. Travel even under the best conditions was slow, while in winter, with the canals frozen, it was nonexistent. For instance:

> The stationary engines on the Portage were stopped on the night of the 31st December, by order of the Principal Engineer. On the afternoon of that day two trains of cars came to this place from the mountain, the last for the season. The navigation closed at this place on the 30th. It was still open at Johnstown on the morning of the 30th, and two boats were expected to arrive from Pittsburgh before its closing. The snow is about 5 inches deep on the mountain, and two or three inches deep at this place.[2]

Floods, too, were frequent causes of delays, as were the necessary transfers between canals and railroads. Not only were there enough physical difficulties, but gross mismanagement and political interference contributed to the inadequacy of the system. Nearly $18,000,000 had been expended in original construction, and never had its operation come even near a self-sustaining basis. In fact, a debt of $40,000,000 had been accumulated by the time the system was sold.

By 1838 it was becoming very evident that a privately owned all-rail route was the only means of preserving Philadelphia's western trade. And so, on March 6 of that year, as a result of a mass meeting, Chas. E. Schlatter was asked to survey various routes. He reported in 1840 on

[2] Extract from a letter, Hollidaysburg, January 2, 1835.

three possible routes, of which the "middle route," by way of the Juniata and Conemaugh valleys, was considered best. Late in 1845 the legislature was asked at a public meeting to charter such a railroad. About this time, too, the Baltimore & Ohio Railroad, ready to extend its line into Pittsburgh, was also petitioning for a charter (having failed to construct such a line within a previously allowed time limit). Finally on April 13, 1846, an act was passed incorporating the Pennsylvania Railroad with a capital of $10,000,000. On April 21, the Baltimore & Ohio was granted permission to build its line from Cumberland to Pittsburgh *if* the Pennsylvania Railroad failed to fulfill certain conditions of its charter. These were that at least $3,000,000 was to be subscribed, $1,000,000 was to be actually paid into its treasury, and at least 30 miles were to be under contract before July 30, 1847. On July 16, 1847, a contract was let for the first 20 miles west of Harrisburg, and on the 22nd, for 15 miles at the Pittsburgh end. As the required amount of subscription and cash paid in was complied with on time, the Baltimore & Ohio rights were declared null and void on August 2. The actual charter dates from February 25, 1847. One of the provisions was that the State could purchase the road at the end of any twenty-year period, this being canceled when the State Works were purchased by the Pennsylvania Railroad in 1857.

John Edgar Thomson was appointed Chief Engineer of the road on April 9, 1847, and under his direction the construction was carried on. The first division, from Harrisburg to Lewistown, 61 miles, was opened for traffic in connection with the canal and turnpike on September 1, 1849. By December 24 of the same year it was completed to McVeytown, 72 miles from Harrisburg. The following April 1, it had reached Sheaffer's viaduct, 85 miles, and on June 10 was at Huntington, 97 miles from Harrisburg. September 17 found the end of track at Mountain House, a mile east of Hollidaysburg, and finally, on October 1, 1850, connection was made with the Allegheny Portage Railroad.

At the western end, the line was finished from Pittsburgh to a point 21 miles west of Johnstown by August 1851, leaving only 28 more miles to be completed. The red-letter day was December 10, 1852, when the first through train from Philadelphia to Pittsburgh was operated over the Philadelphia & Columbia Railroad, the Pennsylvania Railroad, and the Allegheny Portage Railroad. Obtaining the right to operate its equipment over the Philadelphia & Columbia in March 1853, the Pennsylvania Railroad built its own station at 11th and Market Streets in Philadelphia, this being opened May 20, 1854. By February 15, 1854, the Pennsylvania's own track over the mountains was completed and formally opened, after which three trains a day were put into service in each direction, the trip from Philadelphia to Pittsburgh taking from 13 to 17 hours.

Probably the first privately built railroad acquired by the Pennsylvania was the Harrisburg, Portsmouth, Mt. Joy & Lancaster Railroad, which was chartered in 1832 and whose first president was James Buchanan. Before completion of its own line, the Pennsylvania Railroad on November 1, 1848, contracted with this road to operate it for 20 years, and this agreement was later changed to a 999-year lease. It connected with its own line at Harrisburg and with the Philadelphia & Columbia at Dillersville, west of Lancaster.

With the Pennsylvania Railroad completed, the situation in regard to the State Works which had created the Pennsylvania Railroad was now further aggravated by competition. So it was only natural that, in order to dispose of the unprofitable burden, the people of the state started a movement to sell the entire State System. On April 24, 1854, the state offered it for sale at $20,000,000, but no one could be interested in the proposition, nor were there any bids a year later, when the figure had been officially reduced to half that amount.

Finally, a third act was passed on May 16, 1857, offering the system for $7,500,000. A provision was made at the same time stipulating that if the Pennsylvania Railroad was the purchaser, it would be thereafter relieved of freight tonnage taxes then levied, for a payment of $1,500,000 additional. On June 27, the State Works were officially put up for sale and the Pennsylvania Railroad purchased them for the advertised amount, taking possession on August 1. For nearly a year following this acquisition, the Pennsylvania Railroad used the New Portage Railroad tracks while its own through line was being completed, and service was greatly improved. July 18, 1858, saw the first Pennsylvania train make the trip over its own tracks all the way from Philadelphia to Pittsburgh.

Camden & Amboy Rail Road & Delaware & Raritan Canal Cos.

In 1815 the State of New Jersey granted a charter to Colonel John Stevens "to build a rail road from the River Delaware, near Trenton, to the River Raritan, near New Brunswick," this being undoubtedly the very first railroad charter in American history. But because it was considered wild and visionary, nothing resulted. In 1823 the State of New Jersey appointed commissioners for investigating the feasibility of a canal between these rivers, and their report recommended that the state should undertake this work. A bill was passed authorizing the start of construction, but again nothing was done, and again in 1828 another project of the sort failed to materialize. Meanwhile the proponents of a railroad were also trying to obtain a charter. Finally, early in 1830, a compromise between the two factions was effected and charters were granted simultaneously by the state to both the Delaware & Raritan Canal Co. and the Camden & Amboy Railroad & Transportation Co. on February 4, 1830. By the "Marriage Act" of Feb. 15, 1831, the two companies were united and combined their stock but elected separate officers and directors, keeping their accounts also separate and distinct, and thereby becoming the famous "Joint Companies."

Work was begun on the Delaware & Raritan Canal in 1831, and it was put into partial operation by 1835. Its length was 43 miles, width 75 feet, depth 7 feet, and there were 14 locks, each 110 feet long by 24 feet wide, a total elevation of 58 feet being overcome. A feeder from Bull's Island on the Delaware, 22 miles long, was 60 feet wide and 6 feet deep. All of the project was completed by 1838.

The Camden & Amboy also started construction in 1831, and the portion from Bordentown to Hightstown was completed by September 1832 and from there to South Amboy by the following year, a distance of 34 miles. Early in 1834, the entire line from Amboy to Camden, 61 miles, was finished and the first locomotive run into Camden. According to Benjamin Fish, one of the road's directors, the first passengers— some fifty or sixty people—were taken through from Bordentown to South Amboy on December 17, 1832, being drawn by horses. "On January 24, 1833, the first freight cars were put on the railroad. There were three cars, drawn by one horse each, with six or seven thousand pounds of freight on each car."

After the road from Bordentown to South Amboy was completed, and until the summer of 1833, passengers were brought by steamboat from Philadelphia to White Hill and from there, with two horses to each car, and with three changes of horses, driven to South Amboy. The time for the 34 miles was from two and a half to three hours. In September 1833, the "John Bull" was put on the train leaving Bordentown in the morning and returning from South Amboy about 4 P.M. This was the first passenger train regularly run by steam on the Philadelphia– New York route. Although the line to Camden was opened the following year, and the all-rail route via Trenton and the Philadelphia & Trenton Railroad in 1838, the alternate route via steamboat to Bordentown was also operated for many years following.

The New Jersey Railroad, chartered March 7, 1832, opened its line from the Hudson River to Elizabeth in 1834 and had almost completed its line from there to New Brunswick by the following year. There was much protest by the "Anti-Monopolists" against the Camden & Amboy and Canal Companies and in order to anticipate further opposition, various directors bought up a controlling interest in the Trenton Bridge Co. and in the Philadelphia & Trenton Railroad, and in September 1836 made an agreement with the New Jersey Railroad to build a connecting line from New Brunswick to Bordentown in order to have an all-rail line through from Philadelphia to New York. Because of the financial panic of 1837, no work was done west of New Brunswick until June 1838, but by January 1, 1839, the first through all-rail route between the two cities was put into operation, although there was one break at Trenton where passengers were transferred by stages across the Delaware River Bridge to Morrisville. The following year, the old bridge, built in 1804, was strengthened to carry the passenger cars, thus eliminating this shuttle connection.

In the early '60's, because of the dissatisfaction of the New Jersey Railroad with the terms of their agreement with the Camden & Amboy, it projected another parallel route to Trenton, and the Camden & Amboy in turn considered extending their line to Hoboken. Finally, in 1865, negotiations were started, and in 1867 the companies merged, forming the United New Jersey Railways and Canal Co., ending one of the bitterest battles for supremacy. In that same year the Pennsylvania Railroad, in order to extend its connections to New York, entered into negotiations with the United Railroads. These continued through 1870, and with the final terms of a 999-year lease agreed upon, taking effect July 1, 1871, the formal transfer to the Pennsylvania Railroad was completed December 1, 1871.

Northern Central Railway

One of the country's first railroads was the Baltimore & Susquehanna Railroad, chartered February 13, 1828. The cornerstone was laid August 8, 1829, and work was begun in the fall of 1830. Seven miles were finished by July 1831. Cars were drawn by horses until August 7, 1832, when the "Herald," a Stephenson locomotive, made its first trip. The line was completed to York in 1838. In the early '50's the Northern Central Railway was incorporated, taking over the Baltimore & Susquehanna, the York and Maryland Line, the York & Cumberland, and the Susquehanna Railroad. In 1858 the line from Baltimore to Sunbury, 138 miles, was completed and connection with Pennsylvania Railroad made at Marysville. The company was in poor financial shape and the Baltimore & Ohio acquired a majority of the stock, but by 1861 its holdings were put on the market and the Pennsylvania purchased over 43,000 shares, which, together with others acquired in London, gave it a majority ownership. In 1866 the roads operated by the Northern Central included its own line, 138 miles, the Wrightsville, York & Gettysburg (York to Wrightsville), 13 miles, the Shamokin Valley & Pottsville (Sunbury to Mt. Carmel), 28 miles, the Elmira & Williamsport (Williamsport to Elmira), 78 miles, the Chemung Railroad (Elmira to Watkins), 22 miles, and the Jefferson & Canandaigua (Watkins to Canandaigua), 47 miles— a total of 326 miles.

While the Northern Central thus made connection with Baltimore, only the Baltimore & Ohio had a line through to Washington, and under the circumstance the latter refused to sell through tickets, run through trains, or forward baggage. Thus a road independent of the Baltimore & Ohio was imperative, and the Baltimore & Potomac was formed to build such a road to Washington. The new road being opposed as competitive, the charter provided that it was to be a main line to Pope's Creek, about 73 miles, but that branches not more than 20 miles in length could be built. Thus the present line to Washington originated as a "branch" from Bowie, Maryland, which was placed in service July 2, 1872, and the following year, the tunnel in Baltimore being finished, the line was completed throughout.

Belvidere-Delaware Railroad

The "Bel-Del" was chartered by the State of New Jersey on March 2, 1836, with the provision that if it was not completed and in use in ten years, the charter would be void. On March 4, 1837, the time was extended for another five years, and on February 28, 1849, a resolution was passed which would allow the charter to stand if the road was completed from Trenton to Lambertville or some point beyond. On March 19, 1852, the Camden & Amboy Railroad and the Delaware & Raritan Canal companies were authorized to subscribe for any stock not yet taken.

In 1849 Ashbel Welch submitted the report of his surveys for the line and was put in charge of its construction. The line was opened from Trenton to Lambertville February 6, 1851, to Tumble (26½ miles) in

April 1852, to Milford (35½ miles) in February 1853, to Riegelsville (42½ miles) in December 1853. A special train was run from Trenton to Easton on February 3, 1854, to celebrate the line's completion to that point. The last 14 miles to Belvidere, making a total distance of 65½ miles, was finished Nov. 5, 1855, and connection made with the Delaware, Lackawanna & Western. The "Bel-Del" was acquired by the Pennsylvania Railroad as part of the lease of the United Railroads of New Jersey in 1871.

Philadelphia and Trenton Railroad

This line, incorporated Feb. 23, 1832, had completed its surveys by late November of the same year, a distance of some 26 miles. Starting at Trenton Bridge, the route was roughly along the Pennsylvania Canal to Bristol, then to Harrison's Lead Works in Kensington. By August 1, 1833, fifteen miles of grading had been finished and a mile of track laid between Bristol and Morrisville. This part of the line was completed in November of the same year when the "People's Line" for New York via Bristol was established, using horse power. An engine house at Morrisville was planned August 25, 1834. A trial trip with a Baldwin locomotive was run on October 25.

The road was officially opened a few days later. Perhaps a contemporary account from Hazard's *Register of Pennsylvania* can best describe it.

This road was opened on Saturday, Nov. 1, the whole distance twenty-eight miles. We passed over it in company with a number of citizens, among them several of the commissioners of Kensington, several members of the New Jersey legislature, and several members of the editorial corps of Philadelphia. Governor Vroom was a passenger from Trenton to Bristol. The road commences within a stone's throw of Kensington and passes over a most delightful country, immediately in the vicinity of the Delaware, of which an almost constant view is afforded on one side; while on the other, at this season of the year, the husbandman may be described "binding the corn" or ploughing his fields, and the country for miles in the distance, variegated with well provided farms, country seats, flocks of cattle, and various vehicles passing the road in immediate vicinity. This rail road is perhaps the most level and direct of any in this country. There is not a "deep cut" from the beginning to the end of it, and a splendid prospect for miles is continually before the eye of the spectator. We left Philadelphia at five minutes after ten o'clock A.M. and arrived at Trenton long before twelve, the whole distance being travelled in an hour and a half, including four stoppages. We returned in about the same time, thus travelling, both going and returning, 28 miles in ninety minutes, or at the rate of about twenty miles per hour. The road may be travelled at this rate with perfect ease and comfort, and less jolting than is experienced in passing over the best paved streets in Philadelphia in an omnibus.

We may add, that when the whole route of this road between New York and Philadelphia is finished, passengers may with perfect ease pass between the two cities in five hours—may breakfast at seven in New York, dine at one in Philadelphia, and sup at seven again in New York. The road between Philadelphia and Trenton will open to-day for regular travelling. Two lines of cars will run daily; the first starting from Trenton at half past seven, A.M., and Morrisville at 8, with horses—the second from Trenton at 2 o'clock P.M., and Morrisville at half past two, with locomotive. The first line from Philadelphia will leave at half past 8, A.M. with locomotive, and the second line at two, P.M. with horses. We are glad to learn that Aim's commodious omnibuses have been engaged to carry passengers to the depot, near Kensington. This road cannot fail. It is the interest of every traveller to encourage it, and it will be encouraged.

Philadelphia and Erie Railroad

The Sunbury & Erie Railroad was incorporated on April 3, 1837, with a capital of $3,000,000, and construction was to start by June of the following year. However, as work did not get under way owing to the financial crisis following the failure of the Bank of the United States, time extensions for construction were made to 1840, then 1851, 1858, and finally 1860. The first actual work was done in 1853, and in 1854 the City Council of Philadelphia subscribed $2,000,000. Part of the line was opened that year to Williamsport, by September 1855 to Northumberland, and the first train ran into Sunbury January 10, 1856. By 1859, 200 miles of grading and bridging had been completed, of which 108 miles had rails laid, but in 1860 work was almost at a standstill owing to lack of funds, the company being unable to sell its bonds.

In March 1861 the state legislature changed the name to the Philadelphia & Erie, and early in January of the next year the Pennsylvania Railroad arranged to advance the money required to complete the line, leasing the road for 999 years. In October 1864 the entire line from Sunbury to Erie, 287½ miles, was finally completed.

Pittsburgh, Fort Wayne and Chicago Railroad

Even before the completion of the Pennsylvania's main line its officials began to consider sources of travel and trade from points west of Pittsburgh. The management saw that western connecting lines would act as feeders for their valuable traffic and consequently adopted the policy of aiding their construction whenever possible.

First of the western roads which was later to extend to Chicago was the Ohio & Pennsylvania Railroad, which was chartered in 1848 to build a line from Mansfield, Ohio, to some point on the eastern boundary of Ohio in Columbiana County and from there to Pittsburgh. West from Mansfield the road was to be built through Bucyrus to the western state line. Ground was broken in July 1849, and in 1852 the Pennsylvania Railroad invested $300,000 in capital stock of the company. The line was opened for its entire length of 187 miles from Allegheny City to Crestline, Ohio, on April 11, 1853.

The Ohio & Indiana Railroad was the next western extension. Chartered to build from Crestline to Fort Wayne, Indiana, it was started in 1852 and completed November 1, 1854, the Pennsylvania Railroad again taking $300,000 in capital stock.

The final step in the through line to Chicago was the Fort Wayne & Chicago Railroad Company, which was incorporated in September 1852. A contract was let for construction in May 1852, but little progress was made, only 20 miles to Columbia City being finished by February 1856, when worked stopped altogether for lack of funds. In August of that year the three lines were consolidated into the Pittsburgh, Fort Wayne & Chicago Railroad Company, and with the Pennsylvania's help the line was completed into Chicago on Christmas Day 1858.

Financial difficulties forced foreclosure proceedings, and a receiver was appointed in December 1859. The following year an act was passed by the several states concerned for a reorganization of the railroad. The property was sold in October 1861 to five representatives of the bondholders for $2,000,000. This committee operated the road until reorganization was complete and then transferred the property to the Pittsburgh, Fort Wayne and Chicago Railway Company on March 2, 1862.

For some years the business of the company prospered, and despite its eastward business being promised the Pennsylvania Railroad, its directors attempted to locate an independent line to the east. Thus it happened that the Gould interests late in the '60's very nearly acquired it by purchasing practically the control of its stock, whereupon the Pennsylvania officials quickly acted to make their connections with the Fort Wayne route secure by leasing it on June 7, 1869, for a 999-year term.

In this short sketch it is, of course, impossible to describe all of the small roads which were eventually to be a part of the P.R.R. Some pioneer lines which are interesting for their importance as later being part of through routes or for their early engineering difficulties should be mentioned. Such a line was the Madison & Indianapolis. The first railroad in Indiana was begun in 1836 and partly put into service in 1838. At Madison on the Ohio River, in order to bring the road up over the surrounding hills, about 500 feet high, an inclined plane was built. Its operation was different from those on the Pennsylvania State System, for instead of cables, a rack was used, special locomotives being designed for it. Not until 1858, when the "Reuben Wells" was built, did an engine handle trains on this grade by adhesion only.

The Steubenville & Indiana R.R. Company was chartered to build a road from Steubenville to the Indiana state line. In 1854 half a million dollars' worth of this company's bonds were guaranteed by the Pennsylvania Railroad, and the funds were used to help complete the line between Steubenville and Columbus. Finally completed in 1865, with the Pittsburgh & Steubenville Railroad, the Hollidays Cove, and Central Ohio, it formed a continuous road from Pittsburgh to Columbus—196 miles. Early in 1868, after being sold at public sale, the Pittsburgh & Steubenville was reorganized as the Pan Handle Railway Company, the Pennsylvania Railroad having the principal interest. Later the same year the Pan Handle line, the Hollidays Cove Railroad, and the Steubenville & Indiana were formed into the Pittsburgh, Cincinnati & St. Louis. The Little Miami Railroad was leased by the Pittsburgh, Cincinnati & St. Louis in 1870, thus making connections with Cincinnati possible for the Pennsylvania Railroad.

When the lease of the Pittsburgh, Fort Wayne & Chicago was consummated in 1869, half the shares of the Indianapolis and St. Louis Railroad Company (Indianapolis to Terre Haute) were obtained by the Pennsylvania Railroad. Having already acquired a majority control of the St. Louis, Vandalia & Terre Haute, a new shorter line, the Pennsylvania Railroad then had two connections with St. Louis. This second was kept and the other sold to the Cleveland, Cincinnati, Chicago & St. Louis, now part of the New York Central.

In January 1905, the Terre Haute & Indiana, the St. Louis, Vandalia and Terre Haute, the Terre Haute & Logansport, the Logansport & Toledo, and the Indianapolis & Vincennes were combined into one system—the Vandalia Railroad Company—thus merging all the lines forming a direct connection to St. Louis through Indianapolis.

Philadelphia, Wilmington & Baltimore Railroad

Not only was the West eyed by Philadelphians in the early '30's, but rail connections southward were planned. On April 2, 1831, the Philadelphia & Delaware County Railroad was chartered, as was the Southwark Railroad. In the following year the Wilmington & Susquehanna Railroad was formed on January 18, the Delaware and Maryland Railroad was organized March 14, and this was followed by the Baltimore & Port Deposit. These roads were finished in 1837, the last being completed to Havre de Grace, and on July 14, the line between Philadelphia and Baltimore was formally opened via steamboat connections across the Susquehanna River. All the companies were consolidated into the Philadelphia, Wilmington & Baltimore on February 5, 1838.

The Susquehanna River bridge, 3,269 feet in length, was opened for traffic on November 28, 1866, having cost $2,266,983. Some years later the Baltimore & Ohio nearly obtained control of the line, but the Pennsylvania Railroad, considering its important connections to Baltimore and the South, purchased a majority interest in 1881. In November 1902 the Philadelphia, Wilmington & Baltimore and the Baltimore & Potomac were formed into the Philadelphia, Baltimore & Washington Railroad Company.

Long Island Railroad

In the early 1830's various rail routes from New York to Boston were being considered. Because the Connecticut hills and various rivers to be crossed were believed to be too difficult obstructions, a combination rail and water route via Brooklyn, across Long Island to its easterly end, and by steamboat across Long Island Sound to the Connecticut shore, where connection would be made with a railroad to Boston, was projected. The Long Island Railroad was incorporated April 24, 1834, the route planned being from Brooklyn to Greenport, 94 miles. From there a steamship line was to run to Stonington, Connecticut, where passengers and freight would be transferred to the New York, Providence and Boston Railroad.

Two years previously, the Brooklyn & Jamaica Railroad had been chartered, and instead of acquiring this line by an exchange of stock, as provided for in its charter, the Long Island leased it and on April 18, 1836, began its own construction eastward from Jamaica. The first section was opened for use as far as Hicksville March 1, 1837, and then construction was suspended until 1840 because of the business depression of 1837. On October 15, 1841, the line reached Farmingdale; it then progressed steadily until on July 29, 1844, it was completed to Greenport.

The planned schedule of operation was four hours from New York to Greenport, two hours crossing the Sound, and four hours by rail from Stonington to Boston. For a few years through traffic prospered, but by 1848 the supposed difficulties along the Connecticut shore were overcome and a direct rail line to Boston was opened. Within two years the diversion of traffic had caused the Long Island to dispose of its interest in the steamships and practically abandon the Boston connection, the road by then being in considerable financial difficulty. From this date it became solely a local carrier, and a number of branches and extensions were built.

By the '70's two rival lines north and south of the Long Island and parallel with it were in operation, and competition became ruinous. It soon became evident that this situation could only be remedied by consolidation, and after some years of negotiations this was accomplished in the early '90's. The Pennsylvania Railroad acquired a majority of stock in the Long Island in 1900 in connection with its plans for a Manhattan station, and since 1910 the Long Island has used the Pennsylvania Station. In 1904 electrification was started, and six sections were in operation by 1906. The Long Island was one of the first railroads to use steel passenger cars and the first, in 1927, to use steel equipment exclusively.

West Jersey & Seashore Railroad

The first charter for a railroad in southwest New Jersey, dated February 12, 1831, was for a line to connect with the Camden & Amboy in Camden and run to Penn's Neck in Salem County. This line, which was to have been called the West Jersey Railroad, was never begun. The next was the Camden & Woodbury Railroad, incorporated March 11, 1836, and opened in 1838, but abandoned after a short operation. The West Jersey Railroad (second of that name) was chartered February 5, 1853, and opened to Woodbury on the route of the previous line April 15, 1857, to Glassboro April 1, 1861, to Bridgeton July 25, 1861. Its second link was the Millville & Glassboro, chartered March 9, 1859, and opened 1862. Both roads were combined in 1867 as the West Jersey Railroad Co., this being approved by the state legislature March 18, 1868. The third link was the Cape May & Millville Railroad, chartered March 9, 1863, and opened August 23 of the same year. It was leased to the West Jersey Railroad in June 1868 and later became part of that company. By lease of the United Railroads of New Jersey in 1871, the Pennsylvania Railroad acquired control of these lines. The West Jersey & Atlantic Railroad Co. was projected to run from Newfield to Atlantic City (32 miles). It obtained its charter November 5, 1879, and was opened for traffic June 15, 1880.

In June 1933 the Pennsylvania Railroad and the Reading Company started plans for the unification of their southern New Jersey lines and operation. By the summer of 1935 this work was completed with a new passenger terminal at Atlantic City and the consolidation was named the Pennsylvania Reading Seashore Lines. About 85 miles of parallel road was eliminated and new connections and facilities were built, resulting in a more practical and adequate service for the seashore resorts.

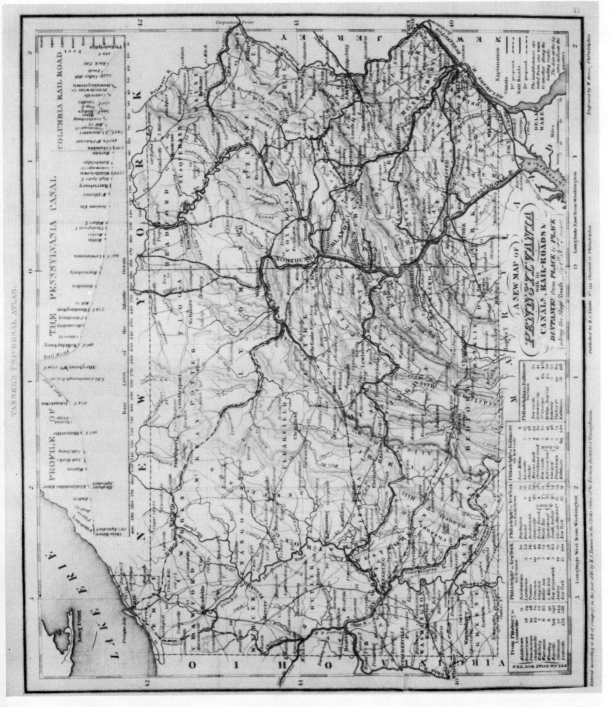

3. Before the Pennsylvania Railroad was built, the State System—part canal and part railroad—was the only route from Philadelphia to Pittsburgh, as this 1840 map indicates.

4. A poster of 1842 depicting travel by sectional canal boats which were carried by rail between canal divisions of the State System.

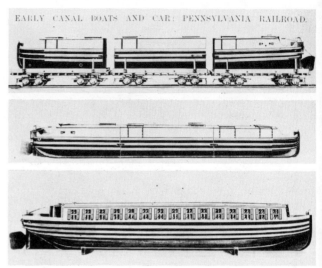

5. Models of the sectional canal boats and a passenger "packet" boat made for the Columbian Exposition.

SCHEDULE OF TIME,
AND
RULES & REGULATIONS
FOR TOWING PACKET BOATS.

FROM PITTSBURGH TO			Hours.	Min.	EASTWARD.
Huling's Station,	11 miles,		4		
Tarentum	10 "		3	45	Pittsburgh to Leechburgh:
Freeport	7 "		1	45	Time, 11 hours and 15 minutes.
Leechburgh	7 "		1	45	
Warren	7 "		1	30	
Saltsburgh	14 "		3	30	Leechburgh to Blairsville:
Tunnel	7 "		1	45	Time, 9 hours and 45 minutes.
Blairsville	10 "		3		
Lockport	10 "		4		Blairsville to Johnstown:
Nineveh	10 "		3	15	Time, 10 hours and 30 minutes
Johnstown	10 "		3	15	
Time through,			31	30	

The above time is intended for the Evening Boat. The Morning Boat must go up at least forty-five minutes quicker than the Evening Boat.

FROM JOHNSTOWN TO			Hours.	Min.	WESTWARD.
Nineveh Station,	10 miles,		3		
Lockport	10 "		3		Johnstown to Blairsville:
Blairsville	10 "		3	30	Time, 9 hours and 30 minutes.
Saltsburgh	17 "		5		
Warren	14 "		3	15	Blairsville to Leechburgh:
Leechburgh	7 "		1	30	Time, 9 hours and 45 minutes.
Tarentum	14 "		3	30	
Huling's	10 "		2	50	Leechburgh to Pittsburgh:
Pittsburgh	11 "		2	45	Time, 9 hours and 5 minutes.
Time through,			28	20	

Drivers must have their teams on the "Tow Path," ready for the Boats when they arrive at the Stations. If not ready, Captains will tow on past the Station, and report all Drivers who are not ready, to the Tow Path Agents.

D. LEECH & Co. Proprietors.

6. Timetable for canal boats on the Western Division Canal of the State System. Westbound boats moved somewhat faster with the current. The "tunnel" was through Chestnut Ridge—1,000 feet long.

7. An interesting poster of 1837 which mentions connections beyond Pittsburgh.

8. A typical old canal lock at Griggstown on the Delaware and Raritan Canal.

9. Remains of the stone block roadbed of the Portage Railroad.

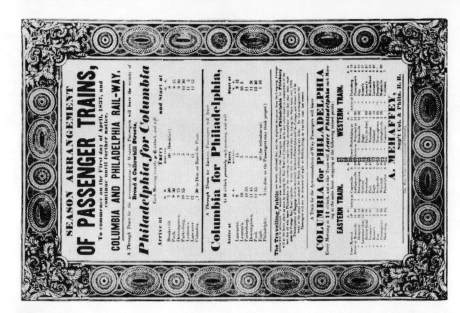

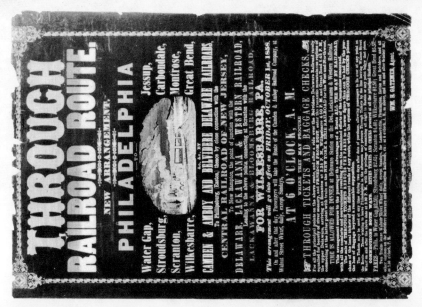

12. Perhaps the first timetable of the Philadelphia and Columbia Railroad, 1837. Previously, horse-drawn vehicles and a few engines were operated on the same rails. By 1836 horses were excluded, and thereafter only locomotives were used.

11. Public notice of the New Jersey prohibition of freight movement on Sundays—1854.

10. A rare old poster of the Belvidere Delaware Railroad giving information about connections with other lines—1858.

13. Lemon House on the Portage Railroad. Here also is shown the building which housed the stationary engines. These, by means of cables, drew trains to the summit of the inclined plane where locomotives were attached. About 1834.

14. A lithograph about 1834 depicting the Belmont inclined plane of the Philadelphia & Columbia Railroad.

15. The station at the bottom of the Belmont plane.

FOG REGULATIONS.

If Fog prevents the 7 o'clock Boat from leaving at 8¼ o'clock, the Boat will not go—the Passengers will go by 9 o'clock Line.   Mr. Head will send 7 o'clock Train at 9 o'clock, from Tacony, if the Boat is not in sight.

If Fog continues till 11¼ o'clock, the 10 o'clock Line will be sent via Camden; and 10 o'clock Line from New York will run to Camden.

If Fog prevents the sending of a Boat to Tacony, after waiting half an hour, send the 8 o'clock Train (from New York) to Kensington.

If Fog prevents the Stevens from reaching Tacony an hour after time, down trip, the Trenton line (Quintons,) will go to Kensington.

If Fog prevents the 4¼ o'clock Boat, leaving at 5¼ P.M. the Passengers will go at 5½ o'clock—And Mr. Head will send Train from Tacony at 6 o'clock, if Boat is not in sight.   And 4½ o'clock Line from New York if no Boat at Tacony, will be sent to Kensington—If Fog permits at 7, Boat will go to Tacony to bring down Line.

When Tacony Lines are obliged to come in at Kensington from New York, Omnibusses will be provided to carry the Passengers to the City at 12½ cts. or 18¼ for Passenger and Baggage.

WM. H. GATZMER, Agent.

November 1st, 1853

16. Passengers traveling between New York and Philadelphia via the Camden & Amboy made part of the journey by boat—at both ends of the trip. This notice shows how fog could interfere with 1853 schedules.

Belvidere Delaware

RAILROAD.

On and after SATURDAY, May 1st,

the lines on this road will run daily, (Sundays excepted) as follows:

The *Accommodation Line* down will leave Lambertville at 5¼ a.m., connecting with the line leaving Trenton at 7 a.m. for Philadelphia.

The *Mail Line* down will leave Lambertville at 2¼ p.m., connecting with the Express Mail line which leaves New York at 2 p.m., via Bordentown, for Philadelphia.

The *Mail Line* up will leave Trenton at 11 a.m., on the arrival of the 9 a.m. Mail Line from Philadelphia.

The *Accommodation* Line up will leave Trenton at 4¼ p.m., on the arrival of the Line which leaves Philadelphia at 2¼ p.m.

FARE—Between Lambertville and Trenton 25 cts.

Between Lambertville and Philadelphia by either of the above lines down and by the Accommodation line up, 75 cts.—by the Mail line up 87½ cts.

EXCURSION TICKETS—Lambertville to Philadelphia, returning same day, $1.25.

On & After MONDAY, May 3d,

An Additional train will leave Trenton, daily, (Sundays excepted) at 7½ a.m., and returning, leave Lambertville at 9¼ a.m.; to continue while the Steamboat makes her regular trips between Lambertville and Easton.

Lambertville, April 29, 1852.

E. VANUXEM, Agt.

17. The Belvidere-Delaware line was still under construction beyond Lambertville in 1852 when this poster appeared. Most early time tables gave departure and arrival times in fractions of an hour rather than minutes, and "lines" was the contemporary word for "trains."

18. A United Railroads of New Jersey train at Vincentown in the '60's.

19. Bingham & Dock, "forwarding merchants," handled passengers and freight for Pennsylvania Railroad from March 1853 to August 1856 over the Philadelphia & Columbia Railroad. This station at 18th and Market Streets, Philadelphia, was jointly owned.

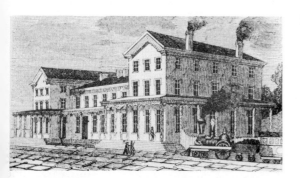

20. Hollidaysburg was the terminus of the middle division of the State System's canal, where connection was made with the Portage Railroad. Here stood the Mountain House, station and hotel. Contemporary artists were obviously not too familiar with railroads, as is evidenced by the ties being shown *on* the rails rather than underneath!

21. An old wash drawing of the arch bridge at Bordentown on the Camden & Amboy in the late '30's. The bell was used to signal the arrival and departure of trains.

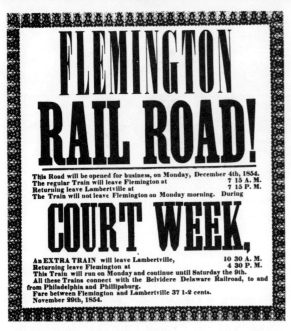

22. Special trains were run in 1854 for Court Week on the Flemington Railroad—a branch of the Belvidere-Delaware.

23. Later part of the Pennsylvania System, the Madison and Indianapolis Railroad originally had no direct connection with it. This 1850 lithograph indicates that river boats were the principal means of travel via Pittsburgh.

24. To provide a direct rail connection between New York and points south of Philadelphia, the Connecting Railway was started in 1864. This extended from Frankford Junction of the Philadelphia & Trenton to the Pennsylvania Railroad west of the Schuylkill River. Some local opposition at the time is obvious from this notice.

25. A rare poster of 1849 giving the schedule for trains between Baltimore and Philadelphia. Although not indicated, a ferry trip was necessary across the Susquehanna River at Perryville.

27. An interesting poster of 1845 which gives a choice of travel—either by ferry from Philadelphia to Camden and then by train to Bordentown, or by steamboat between these points. Travelers for New York would take trains from Bordentown.

26. A New Jersey Railroad & Transportation Co. train leaving Jersey City in the '60's.

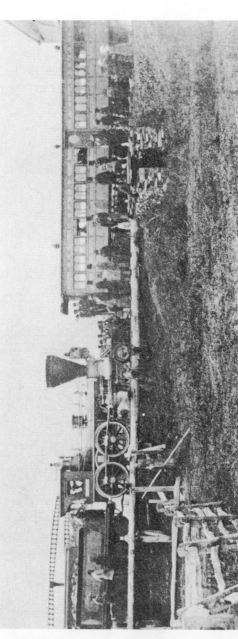

28. The first train into West Chester on the West Chester & Philadelphia Railroad in 1858. The center-door coach is unusual.

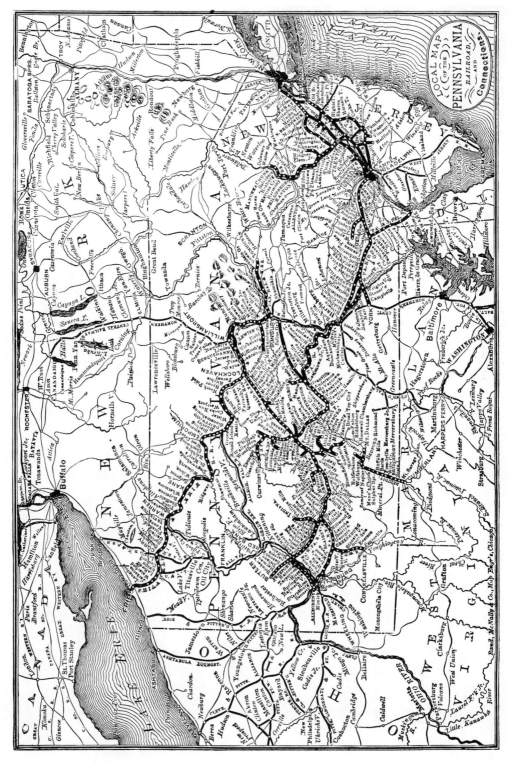

29. A map of the Pennsylvania Railroad just previous to the Centennial Exposition of 1876.

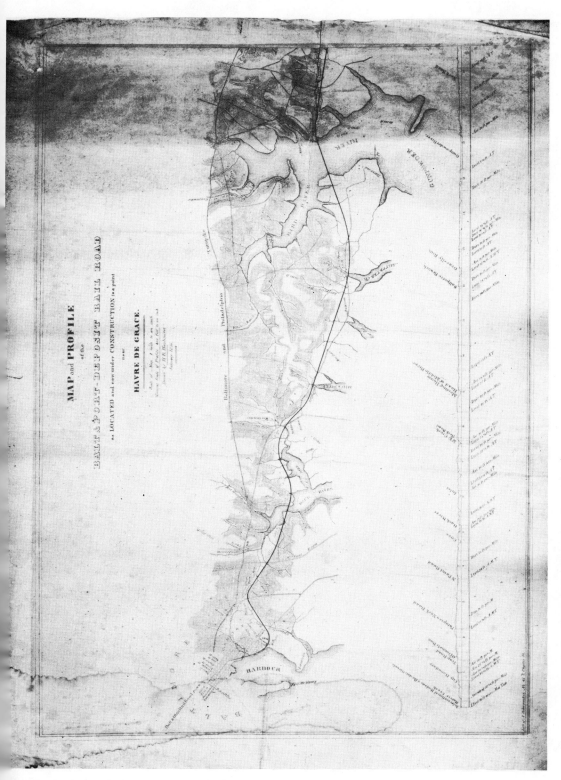

30. Later a part of the Philadelphia, Wilmington & Baltimore, the Baltimore & Port Deposit Railroad was an early forerunner of part of the through line from Philadelphia south.

31. This picture taken at New Brunswick in the '60's shows the combined railroad and highway bridge which was built over the Delaware & Raritan Canal and the Raritan River about 1840. A United Railroads of New Jersey locomotive stands on the bridge.

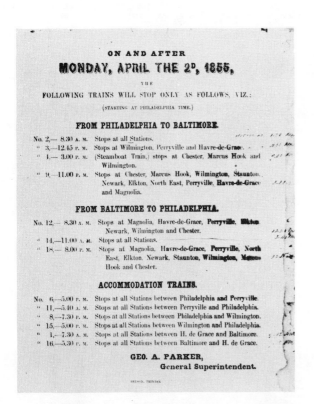

ON AND AFTER

MONDAY, APRIL THE 2D, 1855,

THE

FOLLOWING TRAINS WILL STOP ONLY AS FOLLOWS, VIZ.:

(STARTING AT PHILADELPHIA TIME.)

FROM PHILADELPHIA TO BALTIMORE.

No. 2,— 8.30 A. M. Stops at all Stations.
" 3,—12.45 P. M. Stops at Wilmington, Perryville and Havre-de-Grace.
" 4,— 3.00 P. M. (Steamboat Train,) stops at Chester, Marcus Hook and Wilmington.
" 9,—11.00 P. M. Stops at Chester, Marcus Hook, Wilmington, Staunton, Newark, Elkton, North East, Perryville, Havre-de-Grace and Magnolia.

FROM BALTIMORE TO PHILADELPHIA.

No. 12,— 8.30 A. M. Stops at Magnolia, Havre-de-Grace, Perryville, Elkton, Newark, Wilmington and Chester.
" 14,—11.00 A. M. Stops at all Stations.
" 18,— 8.00 P. M. Stops at Magnolia, Havre-de-Grace, Perryville, North East, Elkton, Newark, Staunton, Wilmington, Marcus Hook and Chester.

ACCOMMODATION TRAINS.

No. 6,—5.00 P. M. Stops at all Stations between Philadelphia and Perryville.
" 11,—5.40 A. M. Stops at all Stations between Perryville and Philadelphia.
" 8,—7.30 P. M. Stops at all Stations between Philadelphia and Wilmington.
" 15,—5.00 P. M. Stops at all Stations between Wilmington and Philadelphia.
" 1,—7.30 A. M. Stops at all Stations between H. de Grace and Baltimore.
" 16,—5.30 P. M. Stops at all Stations between Baltimore and H. de Grace.

GEO. A. PARKER,
General Superintendent.

32. Public notice of the Philadelphia, Wilmington & Baltimore giving stopping times of trains—1855.

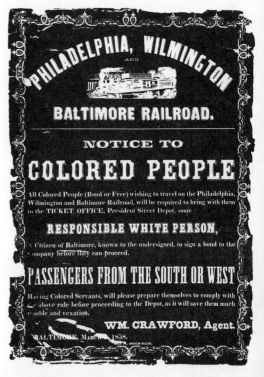

PHILADELPHIA, WILMINGTON

AND

BALTIMORE RAILROAD.

NOTICE TO

COLORED PEOPLE

All Colored People (Bond or Free) wishing to travel on the Philadelphia, Wilmington and Baltimore Railroad, will be required to bring with them to the TICKET OFFICE, President Street Depot, some

RESPONSIBLE WHITE PERSON,

A Citizen of Baltimore, known to the undersigned, to sign a bond to the company before they can proceed.

PASSENGERS FROM THE SOUTH OR WEST

Having Colored Servants, will please prepare themselves to comply with the above rule before proceeding to the Depot, as it will save them much trouble and vexation.

WM. CRAWFORD, Agent.

BALTIMORE, MARCH, 1858.

33. Before the Civil War, to avoid possible lawsuits, railroads were forced to make strict rules for the identification of colored people. This unusual lithograph of 1858 tells its own story.

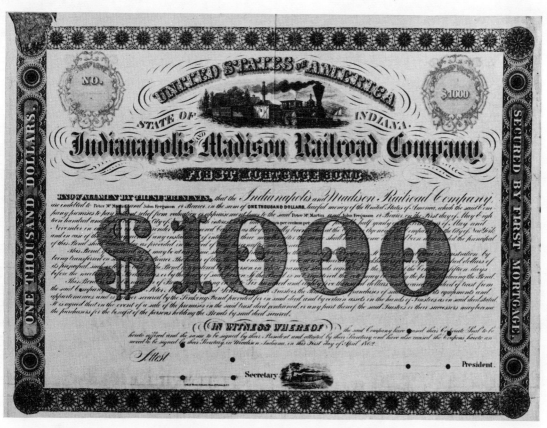

34. A Madison & Indianapolis poster of 1852. Chartered in 1836, this was the first railroad west of the Allegheny mountains.

35. Before final completion of the Belvidere-Delaware Railroad, stagecoaches provided the connection beyond the D.L.&W. in 1856.

36. First Mortgage bond of the Indianapolis & Madison Railroad—1862.

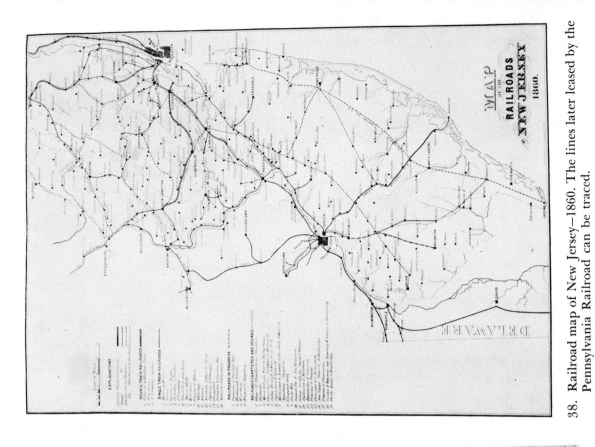

38. Railroad map of New Jersey—1860. The lines later leased by the Pennsylvania Railroad can be traced.

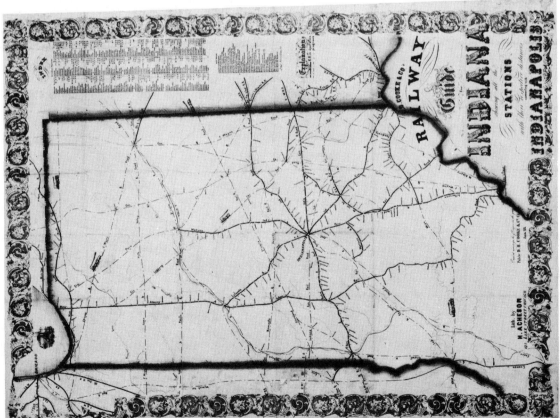

37. Railroad map of Indiana in 1855. As indicated, the Pittsburgh, Ft. Wayne & Chicago was then under construction, and other lines later

M. & I. R. R. TARIFF,
FOR THE TRANSPORTATION OF LIVE HOGS,

FROM.	TO NORTH MADISON. Per Car.	$	Ct.
Indianapolis,		21	00
Greenwood,	"	19	50
Franklin,	"	18	00
Edinburgh,	"	16	00
Columbus,	"	14	00
Elizabethtown,	"		
North Vernon,	"	12	00

FROM.	TO NORTH MADISON. Per Car.	$	Ct.
Shelbyville,	"		
Flat Rock,	"	17	00
	"	16	00

☞ The above Rates are per Car Load, for a Car twenty-two feet long. Larger Cars will be charged in proportion to length.

Rules For Governing The Transportation Of Hogs.

RULE 1. Owners or shippers will be required to receive their Hogs at the Platform at North Madison, and pay Car charges before taking them away. No contracts will be made for transporting Hogs by the head.

RULE 2. An Agent of the Company will be stationed at the Lots at Indianapolis, Greenwood, Franklin, Edinburgh, Columbus, and North Vernon, to whom all arrivals must be reported, the actual number then on the ground, (for transporting,) and the time of arrival. He will keep a book in which all such reports will be entered.

RULE 3. No person will be allowed to report and enter Hogs that are not actually on the ground at the time. And for any violation of this Rule, or imposition practised upon the Agent as to numbers, the person committing it will, upon the Facts being ascertained, be at once placed at the foot of the list, and forfeit his precedence of Hogs then ready for transportation.

RULE 4. No contracts will be made for transporting Hogs within particular times, or on special days. The Hogs will be placed in the Pens in the order in which they arrive on the ground and are reported. If there are more than the Pens will hold, the owners must otherwise provide for the excess until they come in turn. The trains will be loaded from the Pens according to their number commencing with number one, and the Pens again filled according to priority of arrivals.

RULE 5. Owners or shippers will be required to put their Hogs in the Pens according to their entries, under the notification and direction of the Agent; and they will also be required to assist in loading the Cars, so that the Trains may not be delayed.

RULE 6. Should Hogs be placed in the Pens for transportation and be sold out and not transported on this road, they will be charged one cent per head for the use of the Pens.

RULE 7. The number to be put in a Car will be regulated by the owner. Loading will be under his direction except as to time required, which will be left to the Agent of the Company. If one person has several lots arriving at different times, they will be regulated by the arrival of other lots within the intermediate period. To prevent conflicts, lots arriving on the same day will have precedence according to the time of day at which they arrive and are reported.

RULE 8. Whenever a lot of Hogs amount to a car load, the owner will be allowed to furnish one haul; if more than a car load, one hand to every three car loads, to take charge and care of the Hogs while in the Cars. The Company will not be responsible for any loss or damage resulting from smothering or other cause. The Company will not be responsible for any injury the parties may sustain while in charge of Hogs aboard of the cars or trains.

RULE 9. Every exertion will be made to provide Cars for the transportation of all stock, and put them forward with promptitude and dispatch. Further than this, no Agent of the Company will be permitted to pledge its action, and none are authorized to make specific contracts.

RULE 10. Owners or Agents of Hogs are earnestly entreated not to offer or give any donations of money or liquor to the Hands or Agent of the Company, either in charge of Pens or connected with the Trains; and the carrying of liquor on Trains, by persons in charge of Hogs, is strictly prohibited. No hand in charge of Hogs will be taken on the Trains while under the influence of Liquor, and if found intoxicated on the train, or with liquor in his possession, he will be immediately put off.

RULE 11. Hog Cars belonging to the M. & I. R. R. Company, will not be permitted to go beyond Indianapolis unless by special permission (in writing) by the Superintendent.

RULE 12. All persons interested are requested to report all violations—to Rule 10th, particularly.

D. O. Branham,
Supt. M. & I. R. R. Co.

Madison, Nov. 20, 1859.

40. A Madison & Indianapolis Railroad poster governing shipment of live hogs—1859.

PITTSBURGH, FORT WAYNE & CHICAGO RAIL ROAD.
(EASTERN DIVISION.)

Time Table, No. 1,

Commencing on Monday, August 4th, 1856.

☞ STUDY RULES WELL—IMPORTS, &c.—CHANGES HAVE BEEN MADE. ☜

NOTE.—The passing places are indicated by the heavy type, (Flag Stations by a star (*), Big Prairie is a Flag Station for the Mail train. Express trains do not stop at Stations marked thus.

39. An early timetable of the Pittsburgh, Ft. Wayne & Chicago—before completion of the line. This one was in effect in 1856.

PART TWO

THE BUILDING OF
THE PENNSYLVANIA RAILROAD

Rail and Track Development

PERHAPS the earliest important contribution to the art of railroad engineering was the invention of the T rail. Shortly after the surveys for the Camden & Amboy were made in October of 1830, Robert L. Stevens, son of Colonel John Stevens of Hoboken, sailed for England to order a locomotive and rails. At the time, no standard or definite shape of rail had been devised, the various engineers of the early railways here and abroad making their own specifications. During the voyage Stevens spent much of his time whittling wood into shapes of possible cross sections of rails, and finally devised one which he though would serve his purpose. This was the first T rail (or "H" rail, as it was originally called), and for its fastenings he also invented the hook-headed spike. Arriving in England, he had considerable difficulty in getting any iron works to attempt rolling such a design, but at last he persuaded John Guest, the owner of a large mill at Dowlais, Wales, to try rolling the new shape. There were many delays and difficulties at first, owing to the rolling machinery breaking down and the rail coming through crooked and twisted, but eventually the workmen learned how the rail could be straightened while cooling, and the problems were solved.

The first rails completed, according to an invoice of Guest Lewis & Co. dated March 3, 1831, were shipped from Cardiff to Liverpool and there transhipped via the *Charlemagne* on March 28 for Philadelphia, where they arrived May 16, 1831. From there they were sent to Borden-town, although according to old invoices, a number of rail shipments from England went through New York. It has been stated that the rails were 18 feet long, but the invoice says they were 16 feet and that the first lot shipped weighed some thirteen and a half tons, and consisted of 189 bars. The rail weighed 36 pounds per yard and was $3\frac{1}{2}$ inches high, $2\frac{1}{2}$ inches wide on the head, and $3\frac{1}{2}$ inches wide at the base. Later shipments weighed 40 to 42 pounds per yard.

The universal use of wooden crossties came about accidentally. As with other early roads, stone blocks were to be used as rail supports, but when the authorities at Sing Sing prison, who had contracted to supply these, were slow in making deliveries, Stevens ordered hewn-wood cross-ties to be laid temporarily. These were first used in the "deep cut" at Bordentown, and they proved so satisfactory that they were not replaced by stone blocks but rather became the standard thereafter, not only on the Camden & Amboy but everywhere. This was the first track in the world to have the rails spiked directly to the ties.

The first T rail rolled in America was also used on what is now part of the Pennsylvania—the Cumberland Valley Railroad. In 1845 the Mon-tour Rolling Mill was established at Danville, Pennsylvania, especially for making such rails, the rolls being made by Haywood & Snyder and the first rails being delivered in 1846.

An interesting sidelight on early T rails is that in 1848 the Camden & Amboy experimented with the use of 92-pound rail 7 inches high. After this was tried on fifteen miles of the line near Bordentown it was found to be too rigid and was eventually disposed of to contractors for building purposes. This led directly to the later use of I beams for such construction.

A few experimental steel rails were rolled before 1867, but in that year the first ever rolled upon order were made by the Cambria Iron Co. at Johnstown, Pennsylvania. Most of the first steel rails thus rolled for several years went to the Pennsylvania Railroad. Weights up to 1890 ran from 56 to 90 pounds per yard; today, rails in main line service weigh 152 pounds per yard.

Another Pennsylvania Railroad "first" in connection with track construction was the installation of track tanks. The first in this country were on the Pennsylvania lines in the early '70's. These tanks permitted locomotives to pick up water without stopping, by means of a scoop under their tenders. Such tanks are metal troughs about a quarter of a mile long and 6 or 7 inches deep, from which water is taken at a speed of about 45 miles per hour. To prevent the water from freezing in winter, live steam is piped in at certain intervals. The principal reason for their use was the saving of time, as these words from a Pennsylvania Railroad description of 1875 indicate:

> Heretofore much time has been lost by frequent stoppages necessary to fill the water-tank; and, in consequence, express trains had to acquire an extremely high rate of speed between stations to make up for this loss. As now arranged, but two stoppages are necessary between Philadelphia and Pittsburgh—at Harrisburg, after a run of one hundred and five miles, and at Altoona, after a run of one hundred and thirty-two miles, leaving a run of one hundred and seventeen miles to Pittsburgh. Through passenger trains are made up of weight suited to the capacity of the locomotives, and these now average a regular rate of speed per hour over the entire road—the gradients to be overcome presenting no obstacle to the regularity of progress. The fastest trains, therefore, present the paradox of not actually attaining as high a rate of speed as those occupying more time in a through trip.

Engineering Achievements

The Board of Directors early in 1847 appointed John Edgar Thomson Chief Engineer, and under his direction the original route was laid out and its construction carried on. His first railroad experience was with the Philadelphia & Columbia Railroad, where at the age of 19 he worked on its surveys. From there he went to the Camden & Amboy and later became Chief Engineer of the Georgia Railroad, leaving that position for the similar though more important one with the Pennsylvania Railroad. In June 1849, he became General Superintendent, and three years later he was elected President.

Among his capable assistants while Chief Engineer was Herman Haupt, who later held the same position and as such supervised the Allegheny tunnel and the completion of the road to Pittsburgh. To Haupt may be credited the "discovery" of Thomas A. Scott, who in 1852 was the agent at Hollidaysburg for Leech & Co. and who was also to be President of the Pennsylvania Railroad. In the Civil War, Haupt was in charge of construction for the United States Military Railroads; he was also connected with the Hoosac Tunnel construction.

Locating and building the original line was in those days far from an easy project. From the bridging of the Susquehanna River to the famous Horseshoe Curve, through the tunnel at Gallitzin and such picturesque gorges as the Pack Saddle, and down the Conemaugh River, the work was, and still is, an engineering masterpiece. Of all these, the Horseshoe Curve has always been the most spectacular. About five miles west of Altoona in its climb to the summit of the mountain range, the main line doubles back across the Kitanning Valley, forming a great U turn. The rise to the 2,200-foot summit is 92 feet to the mile, or nearly a 1.8 per cent grade. Thus, between the two ends of the U the tracks have climbed 122 feet. Originally only two tracks, the present four-track line still climbs, winding upward around the rugged hills, past Allegrippus and through the twin tunnels, reaching the summit at Gallitzin, having in the 11 miles from Altoona risen 1,015 feet.

From the beginning the main line was planned for double tracks, but some sections were not completed thus until the early '70's, as may be seen in the illustration at Jack's Narrows (No. 43). Then at the start of the twentieth century, through the foresight of Alexander Johnson Cassatt, the Pennsylvania embarked on a vast improvement program, which included four-tracking the entire line to Pittsburgh. Part of this through the mountains entailed a new low-grade freight line using part of the old Portage right of way and making a virtual duplicate of the Horseshoe Curve, known as the Muleshoe. West of the divide, too, between Pittsburgh and Johnstown, another low-grade freight line made the percentage of grade for eastbound traffic only a third of what it had formerly had to contend with.

Much of the original line was relocated, with a saving of miles in some instances; the old canal was filled in where necessary; new bridges were built across the Juniata and other streams; and entire new lines were laid out and built, as at Duncannon. According to a contemporary account of 1903:

> On the western slope of the mountain the engineer who ran the original lines would not recognize the right of way of the present time. The roadbed has been shifted to new sites, the mountains have been cleaved in two, and the topography of the land altered— seemingly regardless of expense—to a suitable path for the modern locomotive. And yet, to the ordinary eye the purpose of all this work resolves itself into the simple effect of securing a level and straight line. . . . The result of all this work will be the greatest railroad in the world. Four tracks the entire distance from New York to Pittsburgh, six tracks for a considerable portion of the way, and two auxiliary roads relieving the sections where traffic is densest, present physical equipment that is matchless in the history of railroads . . .

Bridges

The first great feat of bridging accomplished by Pennsylvania engineers was the structure built across the Susquehanna River a few miles above Harrisburg at Rockville. After it had been started in 1847, the first contract was abandoned, but it was taken up by Helman & Simons of Harrisburg and the stone work of the piers was finished by December of 1848. The superstructure on the Heur plan was the work of Daniel

Stone. In March 1849 six spans of the unfinished bridge were destroyed by a tornado, but nevertheless the structure was completed by the following September 1, when the first train crossed over and went as far as Lewistown. This bridge, 3,670 feet long, carried a single track. On July 17, 1868, five spans for 830 feet were destroyed by fire, and until July 28, when repairs were completed, trains used the Northern Central bridge farther up the river at Marysville.

In 1877 the Delaware Bridge Co. of New York built the second bridge, an iron truss structure carrying two tracks, 3,680 feet in length. This bridge had 21 spans of 156 feet and 2 of 150 feet, using deck-type trusses, three to a span.

The third and present bridge at Rockville was started in 1900, Drake & Stratton building the eastern half and H. S. Kerbaugh, Inc., of Pittsburgh, the western portion. Carrying four tracks, this longest and widest stone arch bridge in the world was completed March 30, 1902. There are 48 spans, each 70 feet long, with a total length of 3,820 feet; the width is 52 feet and the rails are 46 feet above normal river level.

Bridging the Delaware at Trenton is the story of another succession of structures, each reflecting the increasing load capacity required by heavier and heavier locomotives and rolling stock. Here, as the illustrations show, the first bridge carrying the main highway between New York and Philadelphia had five wooden spans. Designed and built between 1804 and 1806 by Theodore Burr, it consisted of two spans of 203 feet, one of 198 feet, one of 186 feet, and one of 161 feet. When the Philadelphia & Trenton Railroad was opened in 1834, passengers were transferred across the bridge by stage coach. A track was laid a few years later, and the small passenger cars were drawn across by horses until in the early '40's the bridge was strengthened so that locomotives could use it. This work, in the form of additional timbers, may be seen in illustrations Nos. 60 and 61. In 1875, because of the increasing weights of motive power and cars as well as the condition of the old spans, a new double-track iron bridge replaced it, and about twenty years later a steel structure carrying two tracks was built. Finally, in 1903 a four-track stone arch bridge, part of the improvement program of the Cassatt era, was completed at a cost of $1,000,000.

Several bridges carrying rails of the Pennsylvania Railroad have been built and rebuilt in Philadelphia. The first bridge used after the Belmont inclined plane was abandoned was that across the Schuylkill at Market Street, designed by Timothy Palmer. The cornerstone was laid in 1800 and the bridge was finished in 1805. It was known as the "Permanent Bridge," as distinguished from the floating or pontoon bridge which preceded it. Built of white pine, it was covered from the weather, the builder saying:

> I am an advocate for weather boarding and roofing, although there are some who say it argues much against my own interests; notwithstanding I am determined to give my opinion as it appears to be right. It is sincerely my opinion that the Schuylkill Bridge will last thirty and perhaps forty years if well covered. You will excuse me in saying, that I think it would be sporting with property, to suffer this beautiful piece of architecture (as you are sometimes pleased to call it), which has been built at so great expense and danger, to fall into ruin in ten or twelve years.

Built originally as a toll bridge, it became a free one when in 1840 the city of Philadelphia purchased it. In 1850, the superstructure was entirely renewed and widened on the north side to carry the track of the Philadelphia & Columbia Railroad, this being operated by the Pennsylvania Railroad a few years later. On November 20, 1875, the bridge was destroyed by fire, severing the connection east of the river. Nine days later a temporary structure was in use and an entirely new bridge was finished in the short period between then and December 24. When Broad Street Station was built, new bridges were also a part of the program, remaining until heavier structures were necessary, being now replaced by a masonry bridge carrying the tracks to the Broad Street Suburban Station.

When the Connecting Railway was completed in 1867, the line crossed the Schuylkill River on the bridge shown in illustration No. 73. This was a combination arch bridge and center iron span which carried two tracks. This iron truss was replaced in 1901 by a steel one, the work being considered quite an engineering accomplishment at the time, as this contemporary account indicates:

The Pennsylvania Railroad never does things by halves, and its latest engineering feat is ahead of anything we have ever heard of, reflecting great credit on its engineers. The bridge across the Schuylkill River just above Girard Avenue, in Philadelphia, is composed of four stone arches, two on each side of the river, and a steel span of 242 feet between them over the river . . . traffic has increased to such an extent, both in frequency and weight, as to make a new span necessary. As this is one of the busiest portions of the Pennsylvania Railroad, and as they always make it a point never to delay a train if it can be avoided, the problem of putting in a new bridge was a serious one. It was satisfactorily solved as follows: False work was built on each side, and in front of both piers next to the span, and the new steel span was put together beside the one it was to replace. The new span has nine sections, and was entirely put together so as to be moved bodily in place as soon as the old one could be removed. Sunday, October 17th, was chosen as the time, on account of fewer trains than on week days, and at 2:53 P.M. the last train, a Chestnut Hill accommodation, passed over the bridge. The last car had just passed over when workmen began tearing away the connections between the span and the pier, and in four minutes the order to move was given. Two hoisting engines with the necessary ropes and tackle started to work, and in two minutes and a very few seconds the old span was out and the new one in place, three minutes more being used to adjust the rails and connections. In twelve minutes after the passage of the last train a special, carrying the engineers, went over and not a regular train was delayed. The old and new spans were moved together to save time, and a total weight of over 1,700 tons was handled at one time, the old span weighing 750 and the new span 970 tons. When it is considered that the span was 242 feet long by 20 feet wide, and was 40 feet above the river, an idea of the difficulties to be overcome can be obtained.

This center span was replaced, 1911–1914, by stone arches (illustration No. 74) and the entire bridge was also widened to carry five tracks.

Connecting the Pennsylvania lines in southern New Jersey with the main line at Frankford Junction is the bridge completed April 19, 1896, across the Delaware River. The center portion comprises three spans totaling 1,944 feet, with a viaduct on the Pennsylvania side 2,129 feet long and one on the Jersey side of 324 feet, making the total length 4,397 feet.

Of the more recent structures, the Hell Gate Bridge is probably the most outstanding, both from an engineering viewpoint and its importance in an unbroken rail link between New England and points south of New York. Designed by Gustav Lidenthal, the span is 1,000 feet long, the top of the arch 310 feet above high water, the towers 250 feet high, and the bridge floor 140 feet above high water.

Because of the nature of the East River at this point, a combination of current, tides, and rough bottom, no support for building the arch was possible from below. It was therefore necessary to build it out from the two towers simultaneously, the projecting sections being counterbalanced by temporary steel stays behind the towers, and all this material was later incorporated into the structure after the arch had been joined. On October 1, 1915, when the halves met, only a deviation of 5/16 of an inch was found. The bridge contains 20,000 tons of steel, and the concrete floor, ballast, and track comprise another 7,000 tons. It was officially opened on March 9, 1917, when the first train from the Pennsylvania Station crossed. This bridge is part of the New York Connecting Railroad owned jointly by the Pennsylvania and New Haven roads, and over it passes not only through passenger traffic between New England and cities south of New York but through freight. This is handled via Bay Ridge, Long Island, and car float to Greenville, New Jersey, eliminating the previous long car float trip to Port Morris in the Bronx, where connection with the New Haven was formerly made.

Perhaps the first of the "long span" bridges was that at Steubenville over the Ohio River, built in 1863 and 1864. The channel span was 320 feet in length and largely of cast iron. Farther down the river, at Louisville, the Pennsylvania Railroad had a large stock interest in the Jeffersonville & Louisville Bridge Co., owners of the first bridge at that point, which was built in 1868–1870 by Albert Fink and consisted of two main spans of 390 and 360 feet. At Cincinnati, too, the Pennsylvania held a majority of the stock and bonds of the Newport & Cincinnati Bridge Co.

In 1890 a new bridge across the Ohio River at Pittsburgh was placed in service connecting the Pittsburgh, Cincinnati, Chicago & St. Louis Railway with the Pittsburgh, Ft. Wayne & Chicago Railway. The method of installing the center span may be seen in illustrations Nos. 67, 68 and 69.

Most modern of the Pennsylvania's bridges is the vertical-lift span at Newark across the Passaic River. Actually this crossing consists of three bridges, a three-track, a two-track, and a single-track, which together carry not only the main line into Pennsylvania Station, New York, but the Hudson & Manhattan tube trains as well as locals into Jersey City. The three-track span, longest of its type, is 230 feet between the bearings, the tops of the towers are 210 feet above high-water level, and the bridge can be raised 111 feet in 85 seconds, giving 135 feet of clearance. Seated, there are 24 feet of clearance at high water. This span was first completed and put into operation March 23, 1935, in connection with the opening of the new Newark Station.

Tunnels

First of American railroad tunnels was that on the Portage road (illustration No. 75) known as the Staple Bend tunnel. It was abandoned when the Pennsylvania built its line and its own tunnel at Gallitzin. Its cost was

$37,500 and its construction shortened the original line by two miles. The first Allegheny tunnel of the Pennsylvania Railroad was 3,612 feet long, the height of the ridge above was 210 feet, and it was arched throughout. The highest point of the tracks was at the western end— 2,161 feet.

Again referring to the improvements initiated by Cassatt, new tunnels were built through the Alleghenies at the beginning of the twentieth century. The low-grade freight line required a new bore to be made. On the main line, too, at Spruce Creek, an additional two-track tunnel was made. Other Pennsylvania Railroad tunnels were those at Baltimore, the first being finished in 1873, another bore being added later. But of all, the tubes under the Hudson and East rivers are by far the most important. These, too, are a part of the improvements under Cassatt, in whose administration the work was commenced. Years earlier, means of obtaining a direct entry into Manhattan were considered. The evolution leading to the present Pennsylvania Station is shown in illustration No. 79.

In 1874 a tube was planned where the present Hudson and Manhattan tunnels now are, and work was actually begun. Known as the Haskins Tunnel, it was not at the time a Pennsylvania Railroad venture. The work was abandoned in 1880, when some twenty men lost their lives through a "blowout" under the river that flooded the project.

In 1884 a bridge was advocated by Gustav Lindenthal and Samuel Rea to cross the Hudson from Hoboken to about 23rd Street.

In 1890, a colossal bridge was proposed in the vicinity of 59th Street. This would have been, if built, the greatest of all bridges, as it was planned to have 3 decks, carrying 14 tracks and roadways. It would have cost $100,000,000 and would have had a single arch of more than 3,000 feet. It would have served not only the Pennsylvania Railroad but all other railroads reaching the Hudson opposite New York. But the other roads would not co-operate, the location was considered too far uptown, and the cost was prohibitive. It was just a little too large a project for the

Pennsylvania Railroad to handle alone with so much capital involved. The idea has been revived from time to time in the interests of the other lines and may not even yet be considered entirely dead.

In 1892 a scheme advocated by Cassatt was discussed. This would have been a line from a point below Rahway with either a bridge or a tunnel to Staten Island and a tunnel under the Narrows at a depth of 125 feet and 3½ miles long to lower Brooklyn. From the tunnel a double track would be built to Long Island City, and then the East River would be bridged with a terminal near Grand Central. The cost of this plan would have been about $52,000,000 and the line to Philadelphia lengthened 10 miles as well as by-passing suburban traffic from Newark and other suburban points. As a result another tunnel from Jersey City under the Hudson and lower Manhattan at Maiden Lane and then through to Brooklyn was brought up, but it was never considered too seriously. A car float arrangement was a possibility discussed also in '92, but it was likewise shelved. So matters stood at the beginning of the twentieth century when Cassatt, at the suggestion of Samuel Rea, investigated the Orleans Railway Extension in Paris — a tunnel through which trains were electrically operated. From his inspection of this line came the proposition for the construction of a tunnel and electric operation into Manhattan both for Pennsylvania Railroad and Long Island trains, the Pennsylvania Railroad having acquired the latter road a year previously. Accordingly, a commission of six prominent engineers was appointed and the planning of the project proceeded. The necessary authority was obtained from the states of New York and New Jersey, but the Board of Aldermen delayed their approval until December 16, 1901, when the franchise was granted subject to a number of conditions, among which were the requirements that electric power was to be used, and that work was to start within three months after all necessary franchises had been obtained.

Construction was carried on beginning in 1902 through the following years until September 12, 1906, when the first tube was completed under the North River, the other tube being finished October 9. The East River tunnels, having 4 tubes, were completed March 18, 1908, and the Hudson and Manhattan tubes were placed in partial service between Jersey City Station of the Pennsylvania Railroad and Cortlandt Street Terminal on July 16, 1909. On September 8, 1910, the North and East River tunnels were placed in service in connection with the new Pennsylvania Station, and the Hudson and Manhattan Railroad was finished and in use on November 27, 1910, when the entire project was in complete operation.

The length of the underground portion of these improvements is 5.1 miles, 1.5 miles being under the two rivers. At the highest point in Pennsylvania Station the tracks are 9 feet below sea level. The tubes were bored through rock, mud, and sand, 70 feet below the river's surface, by the shield method. Compressed air was used to keep out the water, and as the tubes, 23 feet in diameter, progressed, additional rings were put in place. After the tubes were joined, they were lined with two feet of concrete, piping for conduits was built at the sides, and a substantial foundation for the tracks was provided. A third rail was laid and used until 1933, when an overhead catenary system was installed, the tracks being lowered slightly for necessary clearance.

One other important tunnel project in the East is that at Baltimore. In order to bring the Philadelphia, Wilmington & Baltimore through the city and to connect it with the Northern Central and the Baltimore & Potomac, a 3,403-foot double-track tunnel was built in 1873. This served until 1935, by which time, carrying all the north and south passenger and freight traffic, it had become a bottleneck. It also had a 1.2 per cent grade toward the east, and was too small for the electrification planned. Consequently, a new double-track tunnel parallel with the old Union tunnel was built, being completed early in 1935. The old tunnel was then changed to carry a single track and was electrified. Another old tunnel built in 1873 — the 7,500-foot bore of the Baltimore & Potomac west of Union Station — was relined and waterproofed, and also electrified in connection with the other Baltimore improvements.

Signals and Safety Devices

Early signal development on the Pennsylvania was much like that on other roads. Various devices, such as the ball signals (when the ball was raised, the indication was for a clear track) and crude semaphores, were variously used. Probably the first block system was one used on United Railroads of New Jersey between Trenton and New Brunswick in 1863; the first interlocking plant was installed on the same road at Trenton in 1870. For many years the Pennsylvania was the only road using a block system on the line east of Philadelphia.

In the early Pennsylvania Railroad history already referred to, there is a contemporary description of these early block signals, which were manually operated:

As an additional safeguard, the Pennsylvania Railroad Company has adopted the system of block signals which may be described as follows:—The road is divided into blocks between telegraph stations. These blocks are under the charge of the telegraph-operators, who display signals, elevated so as to be plainly seen by engine-men and others in charge of trains—RED indicating danger; BLUE indicating caution necessary; and WHITE indicating safety, or that the track of the block is clear. These signals are operated from both directions, and their use renders it absolutely impossible for accidents to occur by trains overtaking or running into each other. The danger of collision is obviated by the double track.

In 1879 the track circuit and electrical operation was generally introduced and thereafter an automatic signaling proceeded as faster and more frequent trains, congested territory and expanded terminal facilities and yards required. Then in 1915 the position light signals were tried on the main line west of Philadelphia.

These new-type signals were first put into service on the main line between Overbrook and Bryn Mawr in February. They were the now familiar "position light" type, in which rows of lights—vertical, diagonal, or horizontal, indicating clear, caution, and danger—replace color light or semaphore signals. All the lights are one color—yellow. At first, rows of five lights were tried, then four; finally the present arrangement of three was decided upon. A number of conclusions were reached by the initial experimental installation. First, visibility was better in fog, rain or snow, and at night than with other types of signals. Second, with color not a factor, and with several lamps, the indications can still be given even if one lamp is not lit. Third, such signals are more reliable, since no moving parts are involved, and with failures considerably reduced train delays are less frequent. Other advantages are lower initial cost, flexibility of aspects, low maintenance expense, and uniformity of indications. As a result of these satisfactory trials of over twenty years ago, this type of signal has become standard for the Pennsylvania System.

One of the latest developments in signaling on Pennsylvania lines is the cab signal, which gives both visual and audible indications in the locomotive cab, duplicating the trackside signals. These are particularly valuable in snow, fog, and heavy rain when visibility is reduced to the minimum. The installation is so arranged that anything which might break the circuit, such as a train in the next block, a broken rail, or an open switch, will give the proper caution or stop indication in the cab.

Most of the story of modern signaling as applied by the Pennsylvania, including such subjects as interlocking, automatic block signals, maintenance, reverse signaling, and similar devices and operations, must be passed over for lack of space, but their importance cannot be minimized. A few words about CTC—Centralized Track Control—are in order, for with its installation it has been possible to speed and control traffic to an extent which would not otherwise have been possible.

The first installation was at Limedale on the St. Louis Division in 1930, and now some 360 miles of track at fourteen vital locations are thus controlled. CTC materially increases track capacity, eliminates the necessity for written train orders, allows "running meets," puts the operation of all switches and signals for long stretches of track under the control of a single operator, makes the hand operation of switches unnecessary, and gives existing track conditions by means of a track model. Considerable responsibility is attached to the operation of such a CTC machine—or, for that matter, any interlocking plant. A combination of both, such as at Perryville Tower on the Maryland Division, is described in the *Mutual Magazine:*

> Just south of the tower the main line crosses the Susquehanna River on a drawbridge which allows space for only two tracks. On either side of the bridge the tracks fan out into interlockings.
>
> The bridge is manipulated from a point on the structure itself but governed by the operator at Perryville. When a boat approaches the bridge and signifies by three whistle blasts that it wishes to pass through, the bridge operator calls the tower operator, who in turn relays the information to the train dispatcher in Baltimore. Acting on the latter's authorization, the Perryville operator then manipulates a lever permitting the drawbridge to be moved. In so doing he not only allows the bridge to be opened but before doing so also automatically blocks off all traffic approaching it from either direction.
>
> Supervision over the operation of the Susquehanna Drawbridge represents only a small fraction of the control exercised by Perryville tower over one of the most heavily used spots on the main New York to Washington line. The tower is equipped with both CTC type and conventional interlocking machines. The CTC type machine controls the territory from the south side of the bridge to Bush interlocking, including Havre de Grace, Oakington, and Short Lane interlockings, plus Principio—north of Perryville. The electric machine operates the Perryville interlocking and an extent of single and double track on the Columbia and Port Deposit Branch.
>
> It took several years to establish the present extent of the control provided from Perryville, which includes reverse signalling, automatic dragging equipment detectors, code change points, the drawbridge control, and other modern signalling, switching, and safety

devices. The entire installation clicks along smoothly, assuring precision and ease of movement for the many thousands of passengers and carloads of freight.

Another important Pennsylvania contribution to the field of safety devices in conjunction with train operation and signaling is the electronic train telephone system. Developed in collaboration with Union Switch & Signal Co. engineers, it was first installed on certain locomotives and cabin cars and block stations on the Belvidere-Delaware Branch in June 1942. It permits the crews of freight trains and tower operators to talk to each other at any time for the transmission of orders and to exchange information about anything connected with train operation. The conductor and engineer can talk with each other as well as with crews of other trains. By using high-frequency currents transmitted through the rails and the wires of parallel pole lines called "carrier" currents, it is unnecessary to use radio frequencies, and these are confined to railroad property. As a result of the satisfactory trials on the "Bel-Del," similar equipment has been installed on several hundred locomotives, nearly a hundred cabin cars, and six towers between Harrisburg and Pittsburgh—one of the heaviest traffic areas in the country. Its use will be a large factor in reducing delays and keeping dispatchers fully informed of train movements, thus allowing more efficient planning.

Latest development of the train phone is that recently installed on through passenger trains—enabling travelers to be connected with Bell System phones anywhere.

41. Conemaugh Station in the '60's showing "stub" type switches.

42. An example of modern four-track roadbed.

43. When some of the main line had only a single track—a scene at Jack's Narrows in the '60's.

44. The Pennsylvania Railroad was the first in this country to use track tanks—as early as 1870. A scoop let down from the tender took up water while the train traveled at a moderate speed.

45. A modern track tank at Radnor, Pa.

46. A picture taken in 1912 showing a train taking water.

47. Official inspection train in 1913. The special car is run forward and, the end being open, a good view of the track may be had.

48. The junction at Dillersville, west of Lancaster, in the late '80's. The track to the right is the line to Harrisburg; the other is to Columbia.

49. Designed jointly by Pennsylvania Railroad and Industrial Brownhoist Co. engineers, this machine is a ballast cleaner. It propels itself, excavates ballast from the track, removes the dirt, returns the stone to the roadbed and levels the renovated ballast to standard profile.

51. A woodcut of 1875 of the Horseshoe Curve.

A very early photo of the Horseshoe Curve taken in the '60's.

. The present appearance of the Curve.

53. The Conemaugh Viaduct in 1869. This beautiful arch had a span of 80 feet and was 70 feet high. A description in 1855 said, "While it can scarcely be surpassed in the neatness and symmetrical proportions of the design, it is as durable as the eternal foundation upon which it rests." Nevertheless, it was destroyed in 1899 by the Johnstown Flood.

54. This view at Allegrippus in the '80's shows the Allegheny Mountain terrain between the Curve and Gallitzin Tunnel. At this point early in 1854 and within a month of being put into service, the locomotive Allegrippus was wrecked. Its engineman always thereafter referred to the scene by the engine's name. When a station was later established at this place, it was similarly named.

55. A rare lithograph showing the Rockville Bridge, which was finished in 1849. A single track was carried on this wooden structure.

56. The second bridge at Rockville was an iron truss type carrying two tracks. It was completed in 1877.

57. The present four-track stone arch bridge, finished in 1902, is the longest of its type in the world.

58. Until 1866, the Philadelphia, Wilmington & Baltimore used steamboats to make connections across the Susquehanna River. For more than a month early in 1852, as this poster shows, it was possible to transfer cars across the river on the ice.

59. The present bridge across the Susquehanna River at Perryville.

60. Built before 1812, this bridge across the Delaware at Trenton had a track laid for the movement of cars from the Philadelphia & Trenton Railroad to the Jersey side in 1835. The parallel iron span can be seen behind the older portion in this 1875 photograph.

61. In 1839 the original wooden bridge was strengthened to carry locomotives, as can be seen in this picture. Shown also is the new (1875) iron span under construction.

62. The Trenton-Delaware Bridge Co. in 1877 assigned trackage rights to the Pennsylvania Railroad for over 993 years. This photograph shows the steel span which replaced the wooden bridge.

63. The present stone arch bridge, completed 1903 south of the steel bridge which was sold to the Philadelphia, Wilmington & Baltimore Railroad. The highway portion was sold to the States of Pennsylvania and New Jersey.

64. Prefabrication of bridges is not a modern form of construction, as this 1869 photo shows. This is the span forming Bridge No. 5 over the Little Juniata River.

65. Hell Gate Bridge over the East River, New York, nearing completion. The first passenger train crossed March 9, 1917, linking New England by direct rail connection through New York to points south of the Hudson River.

66. Crossing the Passaic River at Newark are the newest of Pennsylvania Railroad bridges. Eastbound trains for Pennsylvania Station use the lower level in the foreground, and Hudson & Manhattan tube trains cross the upper span. Westbound tracks are carried on the third bridge.

67. Bridge construction in 1892—the Connecting Bridge over the Ohio River at Pittsburgh. This view shows the center span being floated into place on scows.

68. Connecting Bridge—the center span in position.

69. The finished Connecting Bridge.

70. A beautiful example of both early bridge building and photography. Valley Creek Bridge near Coatesville, Pa., in the '60's.

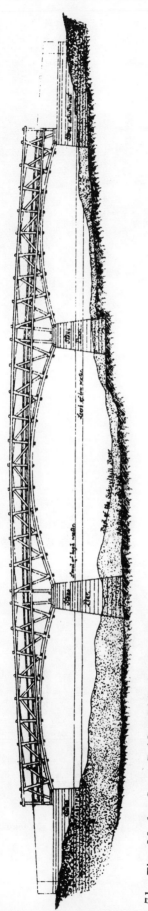

71. First Market Street Bridge, Philadelphia, 1805.

MARKET-ST. RAILROAD BRIDGE.—PHILADELPHIA.

72. Market Street Bridge, 1850, as rebuilt to carry the tracks of the Philadelphia and Columbia Railroad.

73. A train from New York crossing the Schuylkill River Bridge at Philadelphia in the early '80's.

74. Replacing the iron span of the Schuylkill Bridge with stone arches in 1911. This photo shows the work in progress, which included widening to take additional tracks.

75. The Staple Bend Tunnel, the first railroad tunnel in America—built for the Portage Railroad of the State System through the Allegheny Mountains in the early '30's. It was 900 feet in length.

76. A short tunnel at Greensburg in the early '90's.

77. Spruce Creek Tunnel on the main line in the '60's. Now two double-tracked tunnels pierce the hills at this point.

78. Tunnels at Baltimore—the older, built in 1871 at the right.

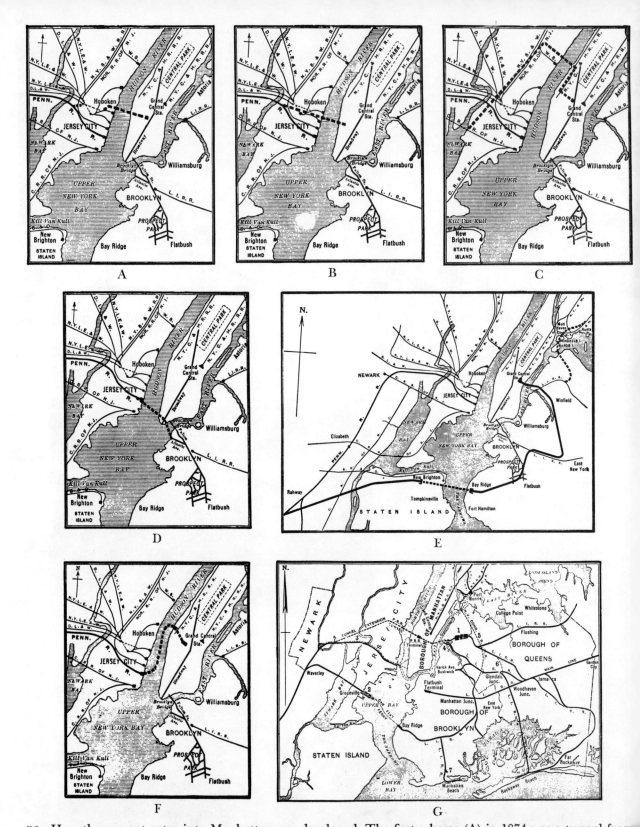

79. How the present entry into Manhattan was developed. The first scheme (A) in 1874 was a tunnel from Hoboken about where the present tubes are located. (B) 1884: A bridge was projected from Hoboken to near 23rd Street. (C) 1890: A bridge was proposed at 59th Street (suggested again a decade or so later by other railroads). (D) 1892: A tunnel under Maiden Lane through to Brooklyn. (E) 1892: a possible bridge or tunnel to Staten Island and a tunnel under the Narrows, then through Brooklyn to a bridge over the East River. (F) 1892: A car float arrangement to carry passenger trains to Manhattan. (G) 1902: The present inclusive plan with Long Island Railroad connections.

81. The finished appearance of one of the tubes of the Hudson River Tunnel.

82. A westbound train emerging from the Bergen Hill portal of the Hudson River Tunnel.

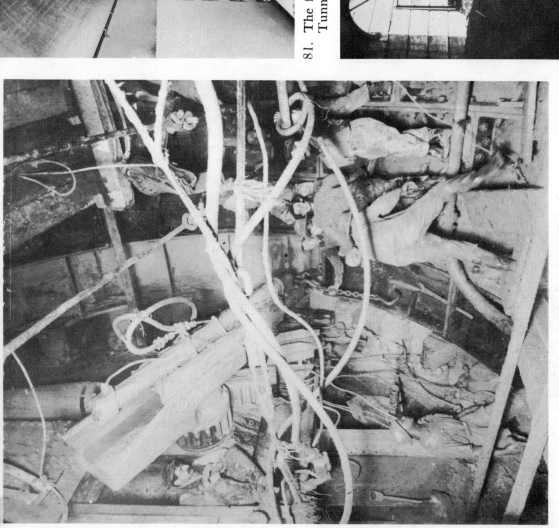

80. Construction work on the Hudson River Tunnel. Work was carried on from both sides of the Hudson and East rivers. The Hudson River tube was joined Oct. 9, 1906, and the East River tube on March 18, 1908.

83. One early type of signaling was the "ball" — indicating clear when raised, though colored balls were also used. Here, on the Schuylkill River Bridge of the Delaware Extension Railroad, are such signals in the '60's.

84. Earliest form of block signal was this non-electrical type in 1875 operated by the towerman and showing red for danger, blue for caution, and white for clear. Instructions for the proper indication were obtained from the operator controlling the next block by telegraph.

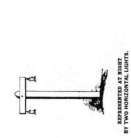

DELAWARE EXTENSION, P. R. R.

AND

JUNCTION RAIL ROAD.

RUNNING

SIGNALS FOR THE GOVERNMENT OF TRAINS

ON THE DELAWARE EXTENSION, P. R. R., & JUNCTION RAIL ROAD.

RIGHT

For Philadelphia and West Chester R. R.
and Philadelphia & Baltimore R. R.

RIGHT

For Delaware Extension
and Junction R. R.

REPRESENTED AT NIGHT
BY TWO HORIZONTAL LIGHTS.

REPRESENTED AT NIGHT
BY TWO VERTICAL LIGHTS.

Schuylkill Bridge Signals:

Red, Stop! White, All Right!

RULES

For use of Penna. Rail Road Tracks, between Junction Rail Road and Market Street.

FIRST.—All Trains running in either direction upon the Junction Rail Road **SHALL STOP** at the Penna. Rail Road connections, and shall not proceed until they receive the proper signal.

SECOND.—All Trains on the Penna. Rail Road will approach connections of Junction Rail Road prepared to stop, if necessary, and be governed by the signals of the switchman.

THIRD.—All Eastward Trains **SHALL COME TO A FULL STOP AT HAVERFORD STREET BRIDGE**

G. C. FRANCISCUS,

Supt. Philada. Div. Penna. Rail Road.

WEST PHILADELPHIA, January 1st, 1864.

85. Probably the earliest form of "position light" signal is shown by this employees' notice of 1864. The instructions are self-explanatory.

86. A signal tower at Lemoyne, Pa., some fifty years ago.

87. Signaling before position light signals — a semaphore about three decades ago.

88. Before signals—a lithograph of a Camden & Amboy wreck in 1855. In this case, one train was traveling slowly on the single track until it met the other, but not in a collision. It was in backing up toward the nearest turnout or siding that it struck a wagon at an unprotected road crossing, with the results shown.

). Interior of tower A at Broad Street Station about 1925.

90. Zoo Tower at one of the most important junctions on the Pennsylvania Railroad. Here traffic from New York and beyond is switched to the south or west or to Broad Street Station.

. Interior of Zoo Tower. The train directors seated at the right give the levermen instructions for routing trains. The machine makes possible "proceed" signals only when switches are correctly set for a train's route.

92. Interior of Tower A, Pennsylvania Station, New York, about twenty-five years ago.

93. Modern position light signals. The lights are yellow and in rows of three. Three vertical light indicate "clear"; diagonally, the signal means "caution"; and horizontally, "danger" or "stop."

94. View in and from the cab of a streamlined **GG-1** electric locomotive. At the left, the cab signal reproduces exactly the appearance of the position light signal seen through the forward window. During adverse weather conditions such as fog, the cab signals are particularly useful.

95. The induction telephone system installed on the Belvidere-Delaware branch enables station agents, towermen, and train crews to keep in constant touch with each other. (A) Station installation. (B) Engine cab telephone. (C) Installation in caboose.

PART THREE

PASSENGER

SERVICE

Stations

NOT MUCH thought was given to station buildings when the first railroads were planned; most of the energy went into the actual construction of the road, and whatever structures were originally planned were first for sheltering rolling stock. A timetable of the Philadelphia and Columbia line of 1837 bears this out in stating, "A through train for the accommodation of western passengers *will leave the vicinity of* Broad and Callowhill Streets . . ." Existing taverns frequently served as stations, and occasionally an inn was built beside the tracks, eventually becoming a stopping place for trains.

Probably the first station in Philadelphia used by the Philadelphia and Columbia Road was the one on the south side of Market Street at 8th Street, opened in October 1850. Another at 11th and Market Streets and at least one other were also used as depots until the Pennsylvania Railroad in March 1853 contracted with Bingham and Dock to handle passengers and freight from a new station at 18th and Market Streets, in which it also purchased a half interest. Passenger cars were drawn by horses to the west side of the Schuylkill River, where they were made into trains and locomotives were attached. A new station built at 30th and Market Streets by the Pennsylvania Railroad in 1864 served as the main depot for some years. It was replaced by another at 32nd and Market Streets, which was opened in 1876, in time to handle the Centennial crowds. This was used until Broad Street Station was finished in December 1881 (illustration No. 117).

Broad Street Station, started in 1880, was the first to have its track approaches above grade. These were carried from the Schuylkill River on a series of brick arches—known familiarly in Philadelphia as the "Chinese Wall." It is soon to be removed as part of an extensive city-improvement program now under way. A double train shed, each shed having four tracks, was built, and the building proper had a frontage on Broad Street of 193 feet and a depth of 122 feet. Within ten years traffic had so increased that this terminal was inadequate, and in 1893 an additional building 14 stories high was finished south of the original structure extending to Market Street. At the same time a new train shed 707 feet long and 306 feet wide was added, covering 16 tracks. One of the country's busiest stations for over half a century, it will soon be a memory when the improvements mentioned are carried out. Then all traffic to the center of Philadelphia will use the present suburban station and the new 30th Street Station will become the city's principal passenger depot.

In March 1927, preparations got under way for the construction of the new suburban station. These consisted of the razing of buildings along Filbert Street. The actual construction began July 28, 1927, and the station was completed and put into use September 28, 1930. The concourse is 1,000 feet long and 200 feet wide, and there are four 1,100-foot platforms with seven tracks—which, when the old Broad Street Station is closed, may be increased to nine or twelve.

Construction began on the 30th Street Station in April 1931. First completed were the upper-level, suburban tracks and platforms, which were put into service at the same time as the Suburban Station, on September 28, 1930. The old West Philadelphia Station closed officially on March 12, 1933, and for eight months thereafter trains were operated on two through tracks below the new station, which was for this time partially open. It was finished and officially opened December 15, 1933. The building is 638 feet long and 328 feet wide, the main concourse being 295 feet by 134 feet, with a ceiling 97 feet high. In a 24-hour period some 511 trains were originally scheduled through the 30th Street

Station, but many more can be and have been handled. With the Market Street Elevated underground (the work is at last under way as this is written), the new West River Drive completed, and the Pennsylvania Boulevard replacing the old "Chinese Wall," the new station will have a setting deserving of its architectural beauty and will be better able to serve the patrons for whom it was planned.

The illustrations of the old stations and, in some cases, of later or present buildings, tell the story of development better than words. Some were amply planned for years to come, others, such as the one at Columbus (illustration No. 107) were adequate for only a decade or so. Fire, too, often led to a new structure, such as that at Alliance (illustration No. 98). One of the earliest illustrations (No. 99) shows Rahway soon after the railroad reached it with a typical train of the period of the early '40's. Following it is a photograph of fifty years later, when the main line to New York crossed Rahway's streets at grade. The present new station not only has been raised with the tracks above grade but has high-level platforms. The illustrations (Nos. 110, 111, 112) also show how the Pittsburgh station evolved from the impressive early building of the '60's through the more temporary one built after it was destroyed in the '77 riots to the present station, itself over fifty years old.

Frequently, in the Pennsylvania's earliest days, a hotel was a necessary adjunct to a station and was, more often than not, company-operated. Some served also as resorts. One of these was the Patterson House at Mifflin, where an 1852 description says:

> The Patterson House—named in compliment of a former President—is one that will tempt the traveller from the fatigues of his journey, and being tempted, will obtain a hold upon the affections of the "in'ard man." The table is sumptuous—the dining room cool and spacious—the servants black as charcoal, and polite as a Pennsylvania sun can make 'em. The proprietor, whoever he is, is evidently a learned man in his useful profession. . . ."

Later well-known resort hotels along or near the main line were at Bryn Mawr, Cresson, and Bedford Springs. At Altoona was the famous Logan House (illustration No. 101), opened in 1854 and for many years one of the finest hotels in the United States.

The Washington Depot of the Baltimore and Potomac is illustrated in No. 125. Built in the early '70's, it was located across the Mall at 6th Street. Some thirty years later, as part of the project for improving the city, a new terminal was planned, to be owned jointly with the Baltimore and Ohio and also to serve the lines from the south. Although both railroads had previously intended to build their own new stations, they agreed to co-operate in consideration of the city's benefit, and so the present Union Station was begun.

Built of white Vermont granite, the station building is 632 feet long and 210 feet wide, and the general waiting room is 220 feet long by 130 feet wide—one of the largest in the country. The largest room under one roof in the world is the concourse, containing 97,500 square feet. From this, gates give access to 33 tracks, of which 20 are stub or dead-end tracks level with the concourse; 8 of the remainder, which are at a lower level, converge into a double-track tunnel passing under Capitol Hill and connect with the southern roads. The Pennsylvania and Baltimore and Ohio lines enter from the north (illustration No. 126), in which direction the coach yards and engine terminal are located. Every possible convenience has been incorporated in this terminal, from a Presidential suite to a swimming pool. Large as it is, its facilities have been frequently overtaxed, especially during World War II. Operated and owned by the Washington Terminal Company, whose stock is divided equally between the Pennsylvania and Baltimore and Ohio railroads, it was opened on November 17, 1907, and its total cost has been over $20,000,000.

On November 27, 1910, the largest through station in the world—the Pennsylvania Station in Manhattan—was opened. Architecturally and from engineering aspects, it is by far the most important terminal

of the Pennsylvania System. Construction was started May 1, 1904, and
necessitated first the removal of 500 houses and several churches on the
28 acres the project was to occupy. After excavation—a gigantic task in
itself requiring 3,000,000 cubic yards in conjunction with the Hudson
and East River Tunnels — the first stone of the building proper
was laid June 15, 1908. All the masonry work, consisting of some 47,000
tons of granite, 15,000,000 bricks, and 150,000 cubic yards of concrete,
was completed in 13 months; 27,000 tons of steel also went into the
building, which alone occupies 8 acres. The 16 miles of trackage beneath
the station comprises 21 running tracks with 11 island platforms. One
of the world's largest rooms is the concourse or main waiting room,
measuring 277 feet by 103 feet with a 150-foot-high ceiling. Two other
waiting rooms are between this and the train concourse, which is 341
feet by 210 feet. Below, with the purpose of separating outgoing from
incoming passengers, is another concourse for the latter. Still another
waiting room at this lower level in the northeast section of the station
is provided for Long Island Railroad passengers, for whom also 8 of
the station's tracks serve. Although generally classed as a terminal, this
great station paradoxically is but a stop for through trains to and from
New England and points on and south of the Pennsylvania Railroad—
and so, of course, it was planned. Altogether, the entire terminal development with the tunnels meant an expenditure of $115,000,000.

Sunnyside Yard is as much a part of the Pennsylvania Station project
as the building itself, for here the vitally important work of making
up trains, cleaning, servicing, and repairing of cars, and all the other
essentials of passenger-car operation are carried on. Largest of all passenger yards, Sunnyside occupies an area two miles long by 1500 feet
wide in Long Island City near the East River Tunnel entrance. It has
a capacity of over 1,400 cars and is divided into sections for Pullmans,
coaches, and multiple-unit cars. Here are located the commissary department, as well as Pullman and railroad facilities for servicing everything
pertaining to passenger-car operation.

Because it is not strictly a Pennsylvania station, though it is the terminus for its southwestern connections, the St. Louis Union Station can be little more than mentioned in this summary; however, its importance is not to be minimized. Operated by the Terminal Railroad Association of St. Louis, it was opened in September 1894 and altered somewhat to handle the large number of passengers attracted by the St. Louis Exposition in 1903 and 1904. Some 42 tracks enter this terminal, 32 being in the train shed, the largest number in *any* station. This is the terminus of such well-known Pennsylvania trains as the "Spirit of St. Louis," the "Jeffersonian," and the "American."

The other main western terminal of the Pennsylvania is Chicago Union Station, which was first planned in 1913 to replace inadequate facilities. Construction was begun in 1915, but work was halted by the First World War; after the war it was continued, and the station was formally opened on July 23, 1925. There are 14 tracks on the south side of the concourse and 10 on the north with 3 tracks running through at the east end for switching. The concourse is 269 feet long, 100 feet wide and 111 feet high, and the main waiting room is 245 feet long and 204 feet wide. Actually, there are two buildings, the main one above the waiting room and the other containing the concourse proper, to which is added a seven-story mail building. Approximately 40 per cent of all mail handled by railroads in Chicago passes through the station. The Chicago Union Station Company is owned 50 per cent by the Pennsylvania and Pittsburgh, Cincinnati, Chicago and St. Louis Railroads, and 25 per cent each by the Chicago, Burlington and Quincy Railroad and Chicago, Milwaukee and St. Paul Railway. The Chicago and Alton Railroad is a tenant of the station.

One more important station must be mentioned—the most modern of union stations—the Cincinnati Union Terminal. In co-operation with six other important railroads the Pennsylvania became a partner to this civic improvement program to provide a complete and handsome terminal replacing five old depots. After years of planning, construction began in August 1929, and the terminal was officially opened on March 31, 1933, having cost $41,000,000. For all the improvements, including engine terminal facilities, coach yards, express and mail trackage and the station itself, an area of 287 acres was occupied. There are 16 through tracks and 8 platforms below the 450-foot by 80-foot concourse, and 216 trains a day can be handled over its trackage.

Passenger Cars

Through 1834, passenger cars were generally of the stage-coach type, though somewhat larger, and were hauled by either horses or locomotives. Car bodies of a rectangular shape began to appear in 1835, and some with end platforms but without steps were used on the Portage Railroad. About this time, the Camden and Amboy operated a type of square-bodied car without platforms and with side doors and small windows, and a little later came to use cars with doors at the ends.

"Bogies," or trucks, were used as far back as Trevithick's time in England. The first in America were on the Granite Railway at Quincy, Massachusetts, in 1826. For passenger service, the Camden and Amboy and Baltimore and Ohio were the first to use trucks on their cars. Six-wheeled trucks were introduced on the Camden and Amboy about 1845 and were standard thereafter for passenger equipment until the Pennsylvania acquired the road in 1871. The Camden and Amboy was known for having some of the best passenger cars in its time, and it is believed that the first car with a center aisle was used on its tracks, having been built in New Brunswick in 1838. After experimenting with various types of seats, this line used the present coach arrangement in 1843, and in 1850 the seats were improved by being made with a turn-over back.

Supposedly the first sleeping car ever built was the "Chambersburg," built in 1837 by Embry and Dash of Philadelphia and placed in service on the Cumberland Valley in the spring of 1838 (illustration No. 134). Later the same year, the Philadelphia, Wilmington and Baltimore evidently put more than one sleeping car into service. The *Baltimore Chronicle* of October 31, 1838, said:

> The cars intended for night traveling between this city and Philadelphia, and which afford berths for 24 persons in each, have been placed on the road, and will be used for the first time to-night. . . .
>
> Night traveling on a railroad is, by the introduction of these cars, made as comfortable as that by day, and is relieved of all irksomeness. The enterprise which conceived and constructed the railroad between this city and Philadelphia cannot be too highly extolled, and the anxiety evinced by the officers who now have it under control, in watching over the comfort of the passengers, and the great expense incurred for that object, are worthy of praise and deserve to receive the approbation of the public. A ride to Philadelphia, now even in the depth of winter, may be made without inconvenience, discomfort or suffering from the weather. You can get into the cars, where there is a pleasant fire, and, in six hours, you are landed in Philadelphia. If you travel in the night, you go to rest in a pleasant berth, sleep as soundly as in your own bed at home, and, on awakening next morning, find yourself at the end of your journey. Nothing now seems to be wanting to make railroad traveling perfect and complete in every convenience, except the introduction of dining cars, and these we are sure will soon be introduced.

The time, however, for the sleeping car had not yet arrived, and as there was insufficient patronage they were taken off. The contemporary description would indicate that these cars were the acme of comfort— but actually they, and others to follow until George Pullman originated a sleeper worthy of the name, were crude makeshifts.

The first passenger equipment purchased by the Pennsylvania Railroad was authorized on April 26, 1848, when, according to the minutes of a board meeting, two passenger cars and a baggage car were ordered "to be ready for the opening of the road." Little is known of the type of early equipment, but is generally believed to be similar to that used on the Jeffersonville, Madison and Indianapolis. Such cars were little more than long boxes with a row of six-paned windows on each side. The end platforms were high and without steps and the short-wheelbase trucks had no brakes.

In August 1850, all the rolling stock of the Eagle and Phoenix Lines, consisting of ten passenger cars, three baggage cars and two short four-wheeled cars were purchased by the Pennsylvania. In 1851, three emigrant passenger cars were acquired from Bingham and Dock for $1800, and the next year all the cars (and "good will") of Leech and Company were purchased for $5,000. Some "narrow" cars at $2,050 each were also bought, these having been used on the Philadelphia and Columbia road, where closer spacing between tracks required that the cars be from 18 to 26 inches narrower than those used on the main line.

Wide passenger cars were used for the first time in through trains between Philadelphia and Pittsburgh on July 18, 1858. The same day, the announcement was made that:

> . . . A smoking car has been attached to each through passenger train, and one of Woodruff's sleeping cars to each of the Fast Line and Express Trains.

The "wide" cars were much improved over previous types, the total length being 37 feet 9 inches, width 9 feet, total height less than 8 feet, with the inside height 6 feet 10½ inches at the center and 6 feet 5 inches at the sides. Window glass was only 18 inches by 22 inches, the solid part of the sides taking up nearly half the length of the car, and the doors were only 25 inches wide. This type of coach, with no ventilation, was considered first class in 1858, and when better equipment superseded it, it was relegated to emigrant service.

As with early coaches on all railroads, the first form of lighting was by candles; later oil lamps took their place. Gas lighting was first intro-

duced in 1859, although it did not replace oil for years. After 1863 the
Monitor or clerestory type of roof replaced the former flat roofs of passenger cars. In 1869 a new design of coach was developed and adopted
wherein the monitor roof was extended out to the ends of the car, arched
windows were used, and a cantilever type of body bolster above the trucks
was tried. On January 27, 1870, a contract was made with the Pullman
Palace Car Company for the operation of its cars over the Pennsylvania
lines. By December 31, 1871, the passenger rolling stock consisted of 195
passenger cars, 60 emigrant cars, 55 baggage cars, 4 mail cars, and 49
express cars. These figures represent equipment only on the Pennsylvania
Railroad proper and do not include leased or affiliated lines.

In 1875 a new passenger-car design was introduced having larger
windows, clerestory roof extended to car ends, and improved trucks
with spiral springs in place of the former rubber blocks. These springs
were the result of many experiments, and the design evolved proved
so superior that other railroads soon copied them, following Pennsylvania
Railroad specifications.

In 1877, experiments were made with a form of automatic coupler
known as the Janney type, this being so satisfactory that it was adopted
as standard for passenger equipment. Steam heating was tried in 1879
with an individual boiler in each car; these experiments eventually led
to the present system of heating by steam from the locomotive. In the
same year enough passenger cars had been equipped with automatic air
brakes to make this system standard instead of the "straight air" type
first used in 1869. In 1882, the Janney coupler was still more generally
installed on passenger equipment for all main-line and controlled roads.
In the same year, the first attempt at electric lighting of passenger cars
was made, a car with seven incandescent lamps operating from a battery
being tried between New York and Philadelphia.

The first dining cars were probably those used on the Philadelphia,
Wilmington and Baltimore about 1863 to 1865. These had, however,
no kitchens; meals were prepared at stations in advance. In the late '60's
and early '70's the Pullman Palace cars served meals, and dining cars

through the next few years began to be as necessary as sleeping cars. In 1882 the Chicago *Inter-Ocean* said:

When Mr. Chas. W. Adams of the Pennsylvania Company announced that his line would surprise the country by placing on the track the finest dining cars yet seen in America, he evidently knew what he was talking about. This he demonstrated Saturday afternoon, May 6, 1882, when he placed at the disposal of a company of invited railroad, hotel and newspaper men the new car "Pennsylvania." This car deserves the credit of being the most beautiful, comfortable and well-arranged of all the many dining cars that are attached to trains entering or leaving this city at present. The car is 61' 6" long, 10' wide, 7' 3" high and 9' 3½" high in the center. There are eight tables 3' 4" long and 3' 7" wide. The dining room proper is 24' long and 8' 9" wide. The ventilators at the top of the car are separated to a greater extent than is usual, thus making the ceiling much wider and the car much lighter and cheerful looking.

Above the handsome mahogany the clear-story windows are of stained glass. The clear story is of curl-ash, polished like the surface of a mirror. Four large double silver chandeliers scatter abundant light through the room, reenforced on each side of the car with four tasteful silver sconces that in three branches hold blush red wax candles. Another feature that attracts attention is the exquisite silver adorned sideboard of carved mahogany, plate glass and dark velvet plush. Opposite this buffet sideboard is a wine closet, while in the rear of the dining-room is the wine closet proper, containing a receptacle for ice, over which are wine racks for 125 bottles. Next to this is a parcel cupboard, and opposite a Baker steam heater, and then a large linen closet.

There are four of these dining cars, which are painted on the outside a rich, warm brown, bordered with a broad striking pattern in gold, carmine, black and green highly varnished, inscribed on the side in rich gold letters, "Pennsylvania" at the top, and "Dining Car" in the center of the body, which runs upon two six (paper) wheel trucks. The ornamentation is appropriate to a railroad car; the harmonious colors are massed with effect and detailed with care, and the design is good. Throughout, everything is in taste. The wood of the car is everywhere mahogany save overhead and quaintly carved. Where it is possible, the partitions are inlaid with handsome, heavy plate glass, made non-glittering by beveled edges. The rich Wilton carpet upon the floor is subdued yet strong in color, and woven in unobtrusive pattern. The curtains that run upon silver rods above the windows are of carmine and golden-olive velvet plush, relieved by rich salmon colored cloth, stiff in pattern of gold bullion, veritable cloth of gold. The seats and backs, which are generous and comforting, are upholstered in deep carmine and velvet plush. The seats fold up, as in a theatre, permitting easy ingress and egress, and show on the under side luminous panelings of mahogany.

These cars were designed by Mr. Theodore N. Ely. Attached to each dining car is another, patterned upon a new model. They contain each a sofa, four large armchairs, and four fancy rattan chairs, and some camp-stools permit onlookers to watch card games played between the permanent seats and on the permanent tables. The car being divided for baggage, the partition forms one wall of this smoker's paradise. Against it are two more most noteworthy improvements, a writing desk, provided with all necessaries for letter-writing, and a library bookcase filled with popular books of fiction.

With the increasing use of de luxe trains came another improvement first adopted by the Pennsylvania Railroad—the use of vestibules at the car ends to replace the open platforms. In April 1889, new Pullman equipment having such vestibules was put into service. These were first of the "narrow" type—the width of the end doors between steps—and a few years later the present type, the full width of the car, was introduced.

Using storage batteries which were charged at New York and Chicago, the "Chicago Limited Express" had electric lights as standard in July 1887, and the following month charging dynamos were installed on the train which were operated by steam from the locomotive. In the same

year 36-inch wheels instead of 33-inch became standard for passenger
equipment. In 1889, exhaust steam from the locomotive was tried for car
heating and was found to be the best system so far devised.

To bring these notes on passenger cars up to the twentieth century,
the following from *Locomotive Engineering* of February 1898 pictures
the acme of luxury of the "plush" era:

> Pennsylvania Railroad's new limited train. A work of art—high
> art—in color and tint, study and ornamentation, is the new limited
> train running between New York and Chicago on the Pennsylvania.
> It is made up of seven gorgeous examples of parlor and sleeping cars.
> The first car is of the composite order, having a baggage room at the
> front end, in which is located the electric light dynamo driven by
> a Brotherhood engine. At the center of the car is the buffet and
> smoking room, with portable cane chairs, and lounges upholstered
> in canary-colored leather. The remaining end of the car is devoted
> to the uses of the tonsorial artist and the bathroom.
>
> The dining car has ten four-seated tables, and can, therefore,
> take care of forty devotees of gastronomy at one time. The kitchen
> is proportionately large and well equipped for the feeding capacity
> of the car. The four sleeping cars in the train differ but slightly in
> their interior arrangement, there being two state rooms in some, and
> one in the others; but the color scheme and ornamentation are
> arranged so that the cars look entirely different—as, for example,
> one car has the seats upholstered in dark blue plush, with a lighter
> tint of blue in the heavily embroidered head-rest covers—all making
> a rich contrast to the dark mahogany woodwork; while the state
> rooms are finished in light mahogany and gold leaf, and a light shade
> of upholstering. The next car, by way of contrast, has the woodwork
> in the state rooms of a delicate green and the upholstering in
> damask. The oriental style of magnificence is further heightened by
> the design of the seat arms—which are supported by elaborately
> carved griffins, covered with gold leaf—and also by the varicolored
> jewels in the deck lights.
>
> The observation car at the rear of the trains, is also finished in

dark mahogany. It has six state rooms arranged at one side of the car; these rooms can be used independent or en suite at pleasure; the doors opening through from first to the last if required. Here again is luxury in the most complete sense, each room being finished in different colored wood and upholstering, and each also having its own toilet conveniences.

In the observation end, which takes about half the car, there are movable chairs, lounges, and those double-header, tete-a-tete affairs, which allow the occupants to revel in each others' soulful orbs. At the rear end of this car is the observation platform, about 8 feet square, surrounded by an ornate gold-plated railing.

The exterior of the train is also a dream in color. The body, below the windows, is of a dark green, ornamented with a green border in gold leaf, at the edges. Above the belt rail, all the space, including letter board, corner posts and vestibules, is of a rich cream color, while the window frames are of a mahogany color. Besides the regular train crew, the train is accompanied to its destination by the electrician, barber, stenographer and lady's waiting maid.

The first use of steel passenger cars in America was on the Long Island in 1905. For the Manhattan tunnel and station improvements, all-steel equipment was planned, and in 1907 an order for 500 coaches was placed by the Pennsylvania Railroad—the first large contract for this type of car going to the Pullman Company. This led to Pullman also adopting steel construction from that time on, and thereafter it became standard for all systems. By 1927 the Long Island became the country's first railroad to operate steel passenger equipment exclusively.

An important step in the direction of comfort for Pennsylvania Railroad travelers was taken in 1931, when the first air-conditioned dining car was tried. In the following summer all diners in New York-to-Washington service were air-conditioned, and by 1935, all regular passenger equipment on through East-West trains had this equipment. All new cars ordered, built or rebuilt at Altoona, are, of course, air-conditioned.

A "behind the scenes" activity of the Pennsylvania Railroad in connection with the dining-car service has been the establishment of training schools for stewards, cooks, and waiters at Columbus, Chicago, and New York in 1927 and 1928. Working in a replica of a dining car, they are given instruction which covers the actual supervision, preparation, and serving of meals. The kitchen also serves experimentally in trying out menus and improved cooking methods before they are used on the more than 200 dining cars. Expert supervision, from the master chef and dietitian to instructing chefs and instructing waiters, assures picked men for the dining-car crews, whatever their duties. Only the best obtainable meats, produce, and other foods are purchased.

An innovation of the Long Island Railroad in 1932 was the first double-tier suburban coach. Standard coaches for this service had a seating capacity of 76, while the new-type car seats 120 passengers. Use of such equipment was planned to allow 40 per cent more seating in a train of the same number of cars, to give more satisfactory service, and to make unnecessary longer station platforms. Additional equipment of this type is being placed in service.

There are many more "behind the scenes" developments in modern passenger cars which contribute to safety and comfort, some of which the traveler can see and others of which are not obvious. Structurally, different metals have been tried in car body construction, such as aluminum and stainless steel. Improvements in trucks, such as roller bearings, improved springing, and shock absorbers, have made cars better-riding. In the newest coaches, such as those operated on the "Trail Blazer" and "Jeffersonian," seating is provided for 44 passengers instead of the former 56, allowing more leg room with deeply upholstered reclining chairs. Six-foot-wide windows with shatterproof glass, baggage racks with fluorescent glareless lighting, and air ducts for the air conditioning built in are also features of these modern coaches. Finally, the finish, in pastel colors with stainless steel, aluminum, and plastic trim, together with end mirrors, harmonizes with the chair upholstery—the seat color determining the color scheme of each car. So much for the latest in coaches—more comfort, relaxation, and convenience being provided than Pullmans could offer not so many years ago.

Baggage Service

From almost the first days of railroad passenger travel, some means for the handling of baggage was provided, the necessity having been carried over from the stage coaches. And when the Pennsylvania Railroad first ordered passenger equipment, as has been noted, a baggage car was one of the first three specified.

A few years earlier, the Camden and Amboy had a peculiar type of baggage car—the forerunner of the modern container car. Because of the boat connections at both ends of the New York–Philadelphia journey, baggage had to be handled four times. To save time, a system using closed crates or boxes was put in operation. These containers were about 6 feet long and 4 feet wide and ran on wheels. Into them the baggage was loaded at terminal stations or on the boats, and when connection with the trains was made, they were pulled off by mules and loaded on flat cars at the forward end of the trains. They were also used for bonded freight between the cities, the doors being sealed by customs officers.

Except for the modernization of trucks, brakes, and heating—and the increasing length as well as steel construction—baggage cars have not changed as much as other equipment on passenger trains. The baggage-man's duties, however, are confined to baggage handling, not as in 1865, when Camden and Amboy rules read:

> Art. 29. Baggagemen, while the train is in motion, shall attend a Brake on, or that nearest the Baggage car; they are required to light the lamps or candles, and to see to and replenish the fires in all the Passenger cars of the Train as often as may be necessary while on the route.

Passengers had to account for their own baggage in the early days—to pick it out when it reached its destination. Naturally, frequent losses and claims against the railroad resulted. This led to the system of checking where a metal disk was attached to each article and a duplicate given to the owner for identification. From these the present cardboard checks and stubs developed.

Handling of baggage at large stations has necessitated a number of special features, from chutes and elevators where more than one level is involved, to the familiar hand and electrically driven platform trucks. Proper handling for theatrical scenery too, is often provided, including special long cars (illustration No. 165).

Mail Service

The beginning of the Railway Mail Service dates from July 7, 1838, when every railroad in the United States was constituted a post route by Act of Congress. In the Postmaster General's Report for 1836, he mentions two of the early railroads, later to be part of the Pennsylvania:

> Already have the railroads between Frenchtown, in Maryland, and Newcastle in Delaware, and between Camden and South Amboy, in New Jersey, afforded great and important facilities to the transmission of the great eastern mail.

At first, a small section of a baggage car served for handling mail. It was not until 1862 that the idea of sorting mail en route was conceived. In 1864, Col. G. B. Armstrong became the first General Railway Mail Superintendent, and Col. George A. Bangs succeeded him in 1871. The foundations of the present railway postal service can be credited to them. The development of special cars for handling the mail was rapid (two early ones can be seen in illustration No. 149), but in essentials, the modern steel postal car performs the same service. Improvements in interior arrangements have reached their peak in the newest Pennsylvania mail car, illustrated in No. 158. Careful planning of facilities with the comfort and convenience of the Railway Mail clerks in mind resulted in a design intended to promote increased efficiency in the speedy and accurate handling of mail.

At stations, especially the larger ones, such as New York, Philadelphia and Chicago, where post offices adjoin, special arrangements such as conveyor belts and sorting platforms speed the movement of mail between post office and trains. In New York, for instance, where the heaviest concentration of mail is handled, over ten miles of conveyor belts are used, 19,000 feet of which are owned by the Pennsylvania Railroad. Assigned to the handling of about 150,000 sacks of mail daily are more than 700 of the station's baggage force, who load or unload 250 cars every 24 hours.

Famous Pennsylvania Trains

For a few years before the acquisition of the United Railroads of New Jersey, through trains from Jersey City for Chicago used the so-called "Allentown Route" via the Central Railroad of New Jersey to Allentown, and the Philadelphia and Reading from there to Harrisburg. De luxe equipment, known as the "Silver Palace Sleeping Cars," was the forerunner of still more elegant things to come. With the through connection via Philadelphia opened, the Allentown Route, although actually 12 miles shorter, was discontinued in the spring of 1872.

The Pennsylvania Railroad was the first to put a "limited" train into service. This was operated in 1876 between Jersey City and Chicago. The number of cars, consequently the number of passengers, was limited —hence the name. Five years later the "Pennsylvania Limited" was scheduled over this route—faster than any previously operated trains, the time being 26 hours and 40 minutes. The finest cars yet built were assigned to this train, and it soon became so popular that the running time was reduced to 24 hours. A number of the features of today's trains were introduced, such as electric lighting, observation car, barber, stenographer, and maid service.

The equipment of the "Pennsylvania Limited" in the '80's and '90's has already been mentioned. The next important date in connection with de luxe trains is June 15, 1902, when the "Pennsylvania Special" made its first run. The schedule was 20 hours between New York and Chicago, and the equipment generally consisted of one of the D16-type locomotives and four cars. It was withdrawn from service in February 1903, but again put in service on June 11, 1905, this time with an 18-hour schedule. On the first day of operation it is supposed to have established a speed record that still stands, having reached 127.1 miles an hour running westbound beyond Crestline. The "Special's" "on time" record was remarkable. On November 24, 1912, the name was changed to the "Broadway Limited," and the scheduled time was made 20 hours. The train was named not, as is often supposed, from the famous street in New York, near which it arrives and departs, but from the great broad way of steel of the Pennsylvania. One interruption in its operation came during World War I, when, from December 10, 1917, to May 25, 1919, it was withdrawn because of heavy traffic. The "Broadway," it need hardly be added, is the finest of the Pennsylvania's steel fleet, having the finest equipment from locomotive to observation car. Its present schedule is 16 hours between New York and Chicago.

The train which carries more famous people than any other was inaugurated on December 7, 1885. This is the "Congressional Limited," running between New York and Washington, whose equipment ranks with the best and whose schedule has been reduced to 3 hours and 35 minutes for the 225 miles, including several stops. Often running in more than one section, it is one of the fastest trains in the East.

A Pennsylvania timetable is necessary for a list of other "crack" trains, such as the "Spirit of St. Louis," the "General," the "Red Arrow," and the de luxe coach trains such as the "Jeffersonian" and the "Trail Blazer" in east-west service. To and from New England, the "Senator" and the "Colonial" are examples, while some southern trains operating over the Pennsylvania north of Washington are the "Silver Meteor," the "Champion," and the "Southerner." In equipment, service, comfort, safety, and speed, the Pennsylvania has an enviable record considering the passenger miles operated, and it is looking ahead to even better accomplishments in this branch of its service.

96. Harrisburg Station as it appeared in the '60's.

97. A suburban station about 1870—Bryn Mawr.

98. An interesting and rare lithograph of the early '50's, Alliance, Ohio. Built in 1853, this station was destroyed by fire ten years later.

99. Original station at Rahway, N. J., about 1840—from an old print.

100. Rahway Station in 1892. With the elimination of grade crossings through the town, a new station has recently been built with high level platforms.

101. Altoona in the '60's. Here in conjunction with the station is Logan House, then known as one of the finest hotels in the country.

102. Altoona station about twenty-five years later.

03. Whitehall — ten miles from Philadelphia on the main line in 1869. A very rustic scene at what is now the suburban station of Rosemont.

104. Susquehanna, a picturesque station on the Philadelphia & Erie in the '60's, with identical buildings on both sides of the tracks.

UNION PASSENGER STATION, CHICAGO, ILL.

105. A lithograph (probably in the '70's) of the Union Station in Chicago.

106. The present Union Station, Chicago, opened July 23, 1925, serves, besides the Pennsylvania Railroa four other roads.

107. Columbus Union Depot from 1862 to 1874.

108. Columbus Union Depot from 1875 to 1896.

109. A design for a suburban station in 1882.

110. Pittsburgh Depot in the '60's. This was destroyed by fire during the riots of 1877.

111. Pittsburgh Station in the '80's.

112. The present station at Pittsburgh, built in 1892.

113. Cincinnati Station in the '90's.

114. Colliers in 1892.

115. Baltimore Union Station.

116. Washington Street Station (corner of Broad St.), Philadelphia, in 1892. Originally the passenger depo
of the Philadelphia, Wilmington & Baltimore, it is now used as a freight station.

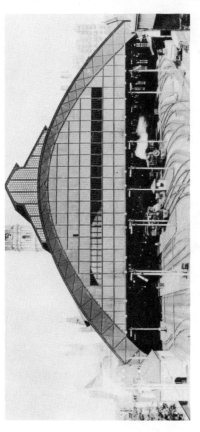

117. Broad Street Station in 1882—shortly after being opened.

118. Broad Street Station in 1888, showing the additional trackage and new train shed.

119. Broad Street Station in 1892—the new building on Market Street. The original building is to the right.

120. Broad Street Station as it appears at present, showing electrification and with the train shed removed (after the fire of 1923).

121. Train gates at the old Broad Street
Station.

122. Mantua Junction, West Philadelphia—where "ZOO" tower is today—as it appeared in the '80's.

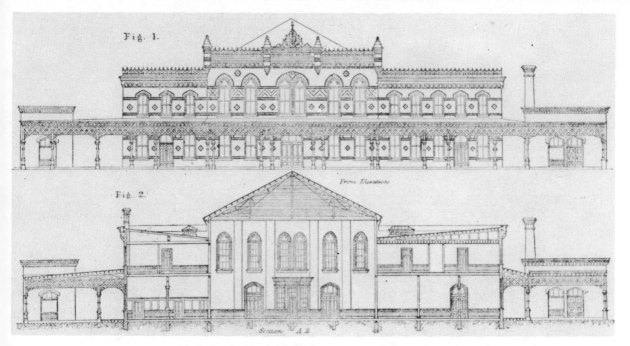

123. Old West Philadelphia Station, built in 1875.

24. The new Thirtieth Street Station.

125. Previous to the construction of the Washington Union Station, this building was the Pennsylvania Railroad terminal.

126. Washington Union Station, completed and opened Nov. 17, 1907.

127. Washington Union Station, from the switch tower. The train to the left is the Liberty Limited just arrived from Chicago.

128. A night view of Pennsylvania Station in New York.

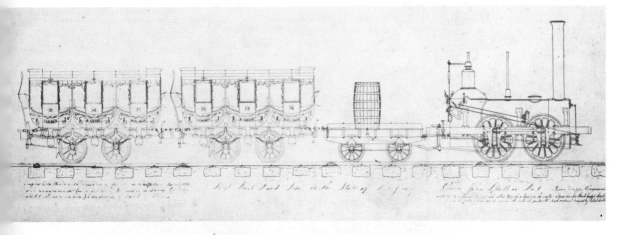

29. An early lithograph of the "John Bull" engine with its train as it appeared when first operated in 1831.

130. This old illustration shows the conditions overnight travelers contended with before the sleeping car appeared.

131. A Philadelphia, Wilmington & Baltimore coach of 1870.

132. Interior of the P. W. & B. coach.

133. A sleeping car of the '70's.

134. The "Chambersburg," probably the first sleeping car ever built. Built in Philadelphia in 1837 by Embry & Dash, it was placed in use on the Cumberland Valley Railroad in the spring of 1838.

135. Interior of the "Chambersburg." Both photos are of a model built for the Columbian Exposition in 1892.

136. Before dining cars came into general use, it was customary for trains to make stops to allow travelers to obtain meals. This A. & P. poster of about 1870 shows a railroad restaurant.

137. Interior of a parlor car about 1890.

138. Interior of an 1890 buffet car.

139. The Pennsylvania Limited in 1890. This was the first de luxe train to have electric lights. A generator operated by steam from the locomotive was carried in the baggage compartment; the exhaust steam is seen above the roof of the first car.

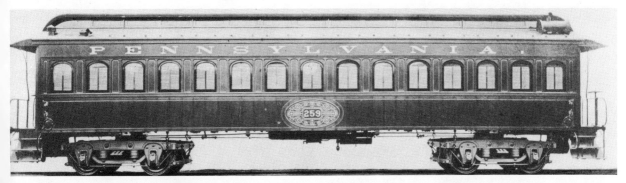

140. Coach No. 259, a car of the late '70's.

141. Interior of an observation car about 1912.

142. An experimental gasoline car of 1910, the McKeen railcar.

143. Modern coaches in the "South Wind," operating between Chicago and Florida.

144. Interior of one of the "South Wind" coaches built by the Budd Co.

145. Interior of the "lunch bar" car in service between New York and Washington.

146. Interior of a lounge car on the Broadway Limited.

147. Interior of the observation car on the Broadway Limited.

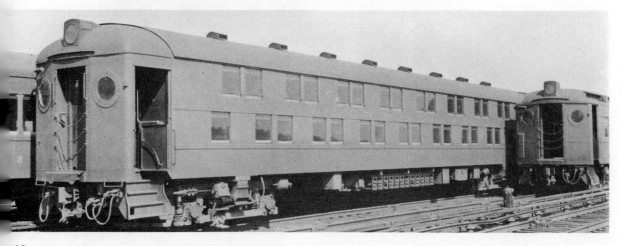

48. To provide more seating for commuters, this double-deck coach was developed for the Long Island Railroad.

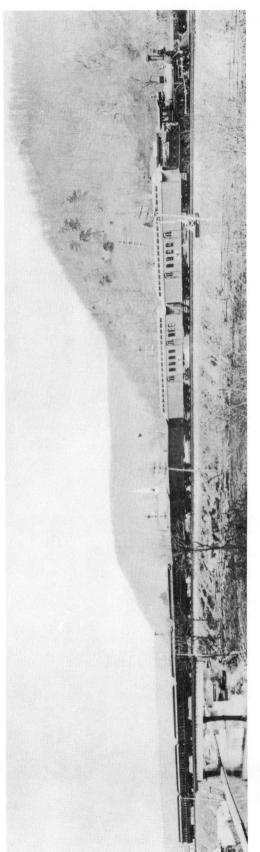

149. The Day Express leaving the Rockville Bridge (about 1885).

151. Rear end of the Pennsylvania Limited of 1892.

150. The Pennsylvania Limited on the Horseshoe Curve (in 1892).

152. A Philadelphia, Wilmington & Baltimore timetable in 1857.

153. A lithograph about 1850-60 advertising Adams Express.

154. An interesting poster of 1856—Belvidere Delaware Railroad, "Trunk Lost."

155. Baggage handling at Broad Street Station in 1911.

156. Loading milk in the '80's.

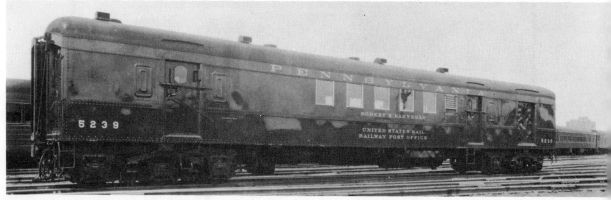

157. One of the latest types of mail or postal cars.

158. Interior of modern mail car.

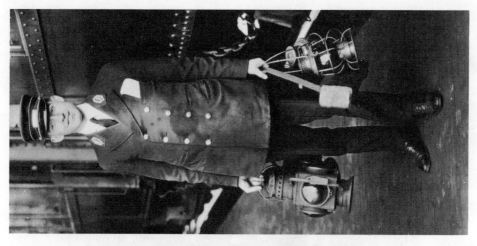

161. Uniforms of trainmen—present.

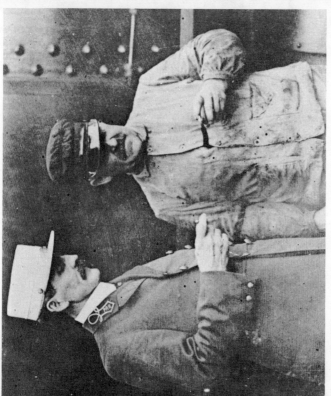

160. Uniform of trainmen—Conductor and engineer in 1911.

159. Uniform of trainmen — a conductor about 1880.

163. Switching a passenger car at Broad Street Station.

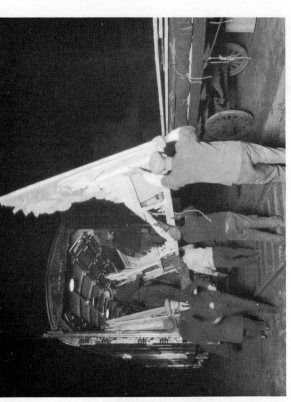

165. The Pennsylvania Railroad has a number of special long baggage cars designed for transporting theater scenery. Here, one of these cars is having scenery loaded.

162. Sunnyside Yard, Long Island City, where passenger equipment is stored and serviced.

164. The cleaning gang washing a Pullman car.

166. The "Jeffersonian" — New York, Philadelphia, St. Louis luxury coach train drawn by streamlined K4 locomotive.

67. The "Broadway Limited," the Pennsylvania Railroad's fastest all-Pullman de luxe train between New York and Chicago.

68. A westbound express climbing "the Hill" near the Horseshoe Curve, in the '20's.

PART FOUR

FREIGHT

SERVICE,

SHOPS, AND MARINE OPERATIONS

ONE OF THE earliest references to "burden" or freight cars is in the report of E. F. Gay, chief engineer of the Philadelphia & Columbia Railroad, to the Canal Commissioners in 1833-34. It is interesting, too, in that it advocates the use of locomotives in preference to horses and also in that it is against the private ownership and use of engines:

You desire such a statement of the practical inconvenience of throwing the Columbia and Philadelphia rail way open as a public highway, as my experience may suggest, I have always supposed that the plan proposed for using the road, viz. The motive power to be furnished by the State, and individuals to furnish cars, and do the transportation, was in effect throwing the road open to the use of the public; but presuming, that, by the word public, you mean indiscriminate use of the road, I shall endeavor briefly to give you such reasons against the measures as my experience will justify.

A railway differs from a common road, in one essential particular, viz: all vehicles travelling upon a rail way cannot deviate from a single track, except at points especially prepared for such deviation, Whereas on a common road, persons travelling are not confined to a particular track, but may accommodate themselves by deviating to the right or left, as may suit their pleasure or convenience; it follows

128

therefore, that upon a railway, when a large amount of trade is done, serious inconvenience must be experienced, unless the rate of speed travelled upon it is nearly uniform..

Upon the Columbia and Philadelphia rail way, if horses should be used, about six hundred cars will be required to do the local and canal trade, of the ensuing season. These cars distributed over the road, would give about four to each mile, travelling each way, per day. There are already about forty private sideings constructed by individuals, at different points on the road, and as many more will probably be put in, which will average about one to each mile; all the individuals owning turnouts or sideings, propose to use their own cars.

The experience of the past season has clearly proven, that burden cars carrying three tons, cannot be drawn at a rate exceeding, on the average, four miles per hour—these facts before us, it must be evident that with six hundred cars on the road, (a large portion of which, will be owned at intervening points on it,) having different hours for starting and different places for stopping, travelling at different degrees of velocity, according to the amount of their loading: there would be no possibility of enforcing any code of regulation so as to prevent the frequent and vexatious collisions and interruptions consequent upon the great variety of interest concerned. Except for speed, rail ways would be of little use. The public would be better accommodated with M'Adamized turnpikes; but for attaining speed, so necessary on an extensive thoroughfare, a railway is decidedly superior, when steam can be used, which indeed I consider the only motive power that should be used upon any rail way over ten miles in length. Should a promiscuous use of horses be permitted on the Columbia railway, the great number of burden cars, and their slow rates of travelling, would necessarily exclude from the road, passenger travelling—which at present, bids fair to become a profitable source of revenue on this rail way.

The idea of allowing individuals to use steam if they please is extremely objectionable, and one if which carried into effect, would bring nothing but ruin to the railway, and be of no benefit to the public, that I deem it unnecessary to make any further remarks in relation to it.

The earliest freight cars were four-wheeled; some were little more than square boxes with side doors. Probably the first movement of cattle by rail occurred in April 1835, when two were brought from Lancaster to Philadelphia and "arrived in one day from whence they started." Before the '50's eight-wheel cars with trucks were common and were generally being built instead of the four-wheel type.

The Pennsylvania Railroad's first purchase of freight equipment was in April 1848, when 75 cars were ordered from Kimball & Gordon.

In 1852, the annual report lists 100 four-wheel box cars, 220 eight-wheel box cars, 96 eight-wheel stock cars and 23 eight-wheel "platform" cars, later called open truck cars. Box cars were termed "house cars" until 1863. By the close of 1856, freight rolling stock totaled 1,861 cars.

"Gravel" and "Powder" cars were listed in 1858 and 1859, the former being classed as wooden "flats" and the latter as wooden "boxes." "Individually owned" cars first appeared in 1863, when the "diamond" type of truck also came into use, although this form of iron truck did not replace the wooden ones entirely for some years. During the same year, semi-elliptical springs were tried on stock-car truck bolsters, the former rubber springs or blocks being removed from above the journals. Brakes were then applied on only one truck of each car. Eight-wheel dump cars were first built in 1868, and "cabin" cars were reported for the first time in 1870. By the following year there were in freight service 2,713 box cars, 1,400 stock cars, 2,762 gondola cars, 1,355 coal cars, and 2 four-wheel cabooses, to which might be added the Philadelphia & Erie's 2,639 freight cars and the Pennsylvania's 1,117 maintenance cars.

Some freight cars were first equipped with Janney automatic couplers in 1882. In the use of these and automatic air brakes, the Pennsylvania Railroad pioneered. All-steel freight cars were introduced in 1898 by hopper gondola cars. Since then individual freight-car capacity has been increased, better braking systems have been installed, better trucks and springs used, construction improved, and special types of cars designed for particular requirements of service—one type, a four-truck flatcar, being capable of carrying nearly 400 tons. At present over 240,000 cars of 50 types are in freight service on the Pennsylvania Railroad.

Freight Yards

Each freight yard on the system has been designed to meet distribution requirements of local freight or to facilitate the movement of through freight. Enola, the largest, is an example. This, on the west side of the Susquehanna River near Harrisburg, is also the world's largest freight yard. It first came into existence as part of the improvement program of the Cassatt era in the early 1900's. Originally having only 12 tracks, it has now grown to have 145 miles of trackage and 476 switches. Here are the most modern devices for expediting movement of freight— loud-speaker systems for crew orders, telephone installations in engine cabs, teletype machines, inspection of the running gear of moving cars from a pit beneath the track, cranes for handling less than carload-lot containers, facilities for necessary car repairs and painting, and an engine house with its 43 stalls and 2 turntables. Within yard limits the eastbound classification yards can accommodate 2,668 cars, and the westbound yard will hold 3,428 cars. The westbound receiving yard can take 1,721 cars, the eastbound yard 1,948, and the container yard 140 cars. Before World War II as many as 10,000 cars were handled on peak days, but during the war, double that number sometimes passed through Enola within 24 hours.

Pitcairn Yard near Pittsburgh is another of the large yards where a variety of freight is handled. Here, too, modern installations such as at Enola speed the movement of freight, an average of 9,800 cars a day and about 88 trains having been handled in wartime traffic. Yards such as these, though not as large, at key points all over the system handle the enormous freight traffic of the Pennsylvania, which constitutes about 13 per cent of the nation's total.

Special facilities for handling different types of freight have been provided at many points on Pennsylvania lines. These include unloading machines, car dumpers, and grain elevators. At Cleveland, Ashtabula, and Erie are docks for unloading ore. Approximately a third of all the ore moved over the Great Lakes is handled by the Pennsylvania. Such traffic is not new (illustration No. 173 shows equipment used in 1892), but the present installations, such as the Hulett Machines at Cleveland, have been a very large factor in supplying sufficient ore for the country's steel mills. The dock at Cleveland was built in 1910 and partially rebuilt in 1939, having a crane runway 871 feet in length, upon which the Hulett machines operate, spanning four loading tracks. Ore can be taken directly from the boat and dumped either directly into hopper cars or into storage piles which are built up for winter use when lake shipping is tied up. Each of the four unloaders has a capacity of 17 tons. Nearly 60 tons a minute can be handled, or a hopper car can be practically filled in that time. From Cleveland alone about 9 per cent of the ore moved by all railroads goes over Pennsylvania tracks to the steel mills.

Outbound traffic from the Pennsylvania by way of the lake ports consists mostly of coal; to handle this, dumpers which empty entire carloads at a time are used (illustration No. 175). From the first freight train operation on the uncompleted main line in 1849, consisting of two trains weekly, this service has developed until now most freight moves on schedules similar to those of passenger trains. Formerly freight was handled from division to division, but the new system put into operation in the 1930's has resulted in the saving not of hours but of days in through freight handling.

Pick-up and delivery service of freight was inaugurated in 1933 and has since grown steadily (illustration No. 186). It has eliminated the extra charges for trucking at each end of a rail movement, permits C.O.D. handling of freight and, of course, exchanges this service with other roads where the same operation is performed.

Shops

When the original line for the Pennsylvania was planned, a site was selected near the base of the Allegheny Mountains for an engine house and one or two shop buildings. The location was chosen because at this point trains from the east were to be broken up or additional engines attached in order to climb the heavy grades. Thus Altoona came to be, and yard and shop buildings as well as house lots were laid out in 1849 and the construction of the shops was begun in 1850. By 1854, when the line was opened through to Pittsburgh, an eight-stall roundhouse and a machine shop, a car shop and a locomotive shop, all in one long single-story building, had been erected (illustration No. 187). From this modest initial establishment has developed the largest group of railroad shops in the world, and with them a large city has also been created.

There are now four large and separate units—so planned for efficient operation. These comprise the Altoona Machine Shops, the Altoona Car Shops, the Juniata Shops, and the South Altoona Foundries. These "Works" employ approximately 11,000 men, including supervisory personnel. The Altoona Machine Shops, now consisting of over 15 buildings, employ about half the total in the Works. They are engaged mainly in the repairing of locomotives and the making of engine repair parts. Until 1868, when the first locomotive built entirely at Altoona was completed, they were used only for heavy repairs and rebuilding of locomotives.

The Altoona Car Shops, consisting of about 12 units, build some of the passenger and freight cars and make heavy repairs to such equipment and to locomotive tenders. Here the first steel passenger cars were built in 1906. The South Altoona Foundries—some six units—make most of the castings from brass to cast iron for the system. The Juniata shops, first planned for the construction of new locomotives, now do largely repair work, some ten units comprising this part of the Works. The latest locomotive shop of the Pennsylvania is one of these units—the erecting and machine shop having four bays and being 691 feet by 347 feet in size. Each of the two erecting bays has a 250-ton electric crane (illustration No. 195), and smaller cranes serve the 50 locomotive pits.

In 1874 a department of physical tests was established at Altoona, a chemical laboratory followed in 1875, and a bacteriological laboratory was built in 1889. The first locomotive-testing plant ever built was put into operation in 1905. It is the only one of its kind in America. In this plant (illustration No. 196) the engine being tested runs on revolving wheels or drums which, in turn, have braking equipment so that operating conditions with trains of varying lengths and tonnage can be simulated. These motive power tests are, however, only part of the present test department, which now occupies more than 50,000 square feet of space and divides its work between pure and applied research and material testing inspection and control.

Together, all the Altoona Works with some 125 buildings and trackage now cover an area of 218 acres—the greatest railroad project of its kind.

Less extensive shops are located at many other points on Pennsylvania lines, such as Wilmington, where most electrical repairs are made, Fort Wayne, and Columbus, to mention only a few. One of these as it appeared in 1892 at Indianapolis is shown in illustration No. 198. In connection with the shops there are hundreds of supply stations where material is stored for ready shipment wherever needed. For example, Columbus in the Western Region is the location of a main store, where, with minor exceptions, all materials for locomotives and cars are distributed. Maintenance-of-way materials are centered at Logansport, Indiana, while air-brake and motor-car repair parts are distributed from Fort Wayne. Elsewhere, as at Conway, near Pittsburgh, old equipment is scrapped, and usable parts are salvaged. This project alone is a major operation; besides the material that can be reworked, the scrap itself is divided into more than two dozen classifications and eventually much finds its way back, remelted to be re-used in new and repair parts.

Besides large shops, most engine terminals everywhere on the system also handle light running repairs as well as cleaning or washing out engines. Originally engine houses were designed only to shelter locomotives (illustration No. 199), but today, this function is only incidental to the servicing. This in a day's operation, usually covers several times the number of engines which might be kept in the building.

Marine Operations

The Pennsylvania Railroad has a "navy" of its own, consisting of some 342 items of floating equipment. The date of its inception is back in the Camden and Amboy days, when steamships were necessary for transporting passengers and freight from Philadelphia to Bordentown and from New York to South Amboy. In 1860 Pier I in New York and Walnut Street Wharf in Philadelphia were the only marine freight depots owned by the Camden and Amboy. In 1866 Harsimus Cove on the Hudson above Jersey City was acquired for $1,200,000 to develop further freight and marine terminal facilities. With the Pennsylvania's lease of the United Railroads a few years later, this property soon became one of the finest waterfront terminals in the country, a description of 1875 saying:

> . . . They have been made at a cost of several million dollars, and probably exceed, in their magnitude and perfectness, anything of their kind on the continent.—Their careful study would well repay all interested in the railway business of America.

With the development of waterfront facilities at New York Harbor, more and more floating equipment was added—principally for freight, including tugs, car floats, lighters, derrick barges, refrigerator barges, and other marine units. From Greenville yard across the Upper Bay to Bay Ridge, Long Island, through freight is transferred, while from both Greenville and Harsimus Cove, local freight to and from Manhattan and Brooklyn Pier stations is handled.

For this part of the marine operations, a fleet of 28 tugboats is in service with 78 car floats, some of which are as long as 330 feet and capable of carrying 20 cars. In lighterage service, where outbound and arriving steamships are loaded and unloaded, 126 covered barges, 20 steam-hoist derricks, 18 open-deck lighters (scows), 8 grain barges, and 6 steam lighters are used. Coal tows from South Amboy to power plants, industries and steamship piers, consisting of 6 to 20 boats, each having varying capacities of 600 to 16,000 tons, are another harbor operation taking place twice daily.

In passenger service there is a fleet of ferryboats operating between Cortlandt Street, Manhattan, and Exchange Place, Jersey City. Formerly service from 23rd Street and Brooklyn was also provided, until the Hudson-Manhattan tubes and main Pennsylvania Station opening eliminated the need for it. Long before the Hell Gate Bridge route was planned, the transfer steamer *Maryland* was used to move passenger cars between Jersey City and Mott Haven in the Bronx. The following news report concerning it is interesting:

> The transfer boat "Maryland," whose name is familiar to many railroad men, was burned at the wharf of the New York, New Haven & Hartford, at Harlem River, near Second Avenue and 133rd Street, New York City, on Friday night December 7 (1888). Two sleeping, one passenger and one baggage car, constituting the regular night express from Washington to Boston, were upon the boat, and there were about 50 passengers in them, many of whom were asleep. The steamer left Jersey City about 10 o'clock and had just arrived and made fast to her slip at 11:10 P.M. when the fire broke out. It originated in the kitchen of the boat and spread so rapidly that the passengers had to flee for their lives, some of them being cut off from access to the shore and escaping only by the aid of a tugboat, which took them off from the outer end of the steamer.
>
> The two sleeping cars were pulled off the boat, but not in season to save them. The woodwork of the boat was wholly consumed, leaving the iron hull bare in the water. The passengers, some of whom were clad only in their night clothes, afterwards held a meeting in the waiting room of the station and passed resolutions appre-

ciative of the good treatment received at the hands of the railroad employees.

The "Maryland" was built in 1853 and was used to transfer the trains of the Philadelphia, Wilmington and Baltimore across the Susquehanna River at Havre de Grace, Maryland. During the war she was used by the Government as a dispatcher and naval supply boat. After the completion of the bridge at Havre de Grace, she was laid up for some time, and in 1876 brought to New York Harbor and put upon the service in which she has since been engaged. The through passenger line between Boston and Philadelphia over the New York and New England, New York, New Haven & Hartford and Pennsylvania, which was then established, and which carried large numbers of passengers to the Centennial Exhibition, has been the only line without change of cars between the termini named, and as there is no other craft immediately available for transferring passenger cars, the line would seem to be now seriously interrupted. In fact, the service has been intermitted once or twice for considerable periods when the "Maryland" has been taken off for repairs. The steamer was of 1,093 tons burden and had track room for 8 passenger cars. She was 230 ft. long by 65 wide, and was manned by a crew of 28 men.

A substitute route was planned before the end of the month for the Boston and Washington express, via the New York and New England Railroad to Fishkill, where it would be taken by boat to Newburgh. From there it would use the New York, Lake Erie and Western to Jersey City, where it would connect with the Pennsylvania and from there over its former route. Later another *Maryland* took over the New York Harbor transfer of the night express train, being operated until the Hell Gate Bridge was opened for this traffic.

Besides the New York Harbor operations, another Pennsylvania "Navy" service is at Philadelphia, where passenger ferries connect with Camden and freight is moved similarly as at New York, though not so extensively. At Philadelphia, however, are special facilities for handling coal, ore, and grain, the three piers at Girard Point having two ore-unloading machines and a concrete grain elevator with a capacity of 2,225,-000 bushels. At Greenwich are two coal dumpers capable of handling 1,200 cars a day. Two floating grain elevators and four grain barges are also in service.

Important marine operations are also carried on across Chesapeake Bay, having originally commenced in 1884. In the Cape Charles–Norfolk and Old Point service are steamers carrying passengers, express, freight and automobiles. Between Cape Charles and Little Creek the rail transfer service is handled by eight tugs, seven barges, and two car floats. Three trips daily are the usual quota for a tug and barge over the 26-mile run, and the time is usually about three and a half hours. Another Chesapeake Bay ferry service is maintained between Baltimore and Love Point as a short cut to the Eastern Shore.

169. Old freight station corner 13th and Walnut Streets, Philadelphia, site of Wanamaker's store about 1870.

CAMDEN & AMBOY RAILROAD AND TRANSPORTATION COMPANY.

FOR THE CONVEYANCE OF MERCHANDISE AND PRODUCE OF ALL KINDS,

TO NEW-YORK, PHILADELPHIA, AND INTERMEDIATE PLACES.

BENJ. FISH, Agent,	Railroad Station, Trenton,	NEW JERSEY
ALFRED DECKER, Agent,	Pier No. 1, North River,	NEW-YORK.
WM. S. FREEMAN, Agent,	No. 46 Delaware Avenue,	PHILADELPHIA.

C446

Marks and Numbers.

TRENTON, 185_

Received *from*

Marked and numbered as in the margin, which we promise to deliver to

or order, at our office, in   upon payment
of freight therefor, at the rate of   cents per 100 lbs.

☞ *The responsibility of the Company as carriers of said goods is hereby limited so as not to exceed one hundred dollars for every 100 lbs. weight thereof, and at that rate for a greater or less quantity, the shipper declining to pay for any higher risk. In case of loss or damage, due proof of the amount thereof to be made by the claimant.*
N. B.—The Company will insure to any amount, if desired.

For the Company.

170. Old receipt, Camden & Amboy.

171. Freight yard at Trenton in 1875. The old four-wheel coal cars were then being replaced by double-trucked types.

172. Piers No. 4 and No. 5, New York, in 1892. An interesting view for comparison with the present city skyline.

173. Ore docks, Cleveland, 1892.

174. Ore dock, Cleveland, present.

175. Ore unloader at Ashtabula.

176. Grain Elevator, 1892.

178. Specially marked cars were operated by the "fast freight lines," among which were the Green, Union and Empire lines. They were originally privately owned and rates were higher than on ordinary freight, the companies assuming more responsibility than the railroads. This photo taken in the '60's shows the markings of cars, the West Philadelphia Shops in the background.

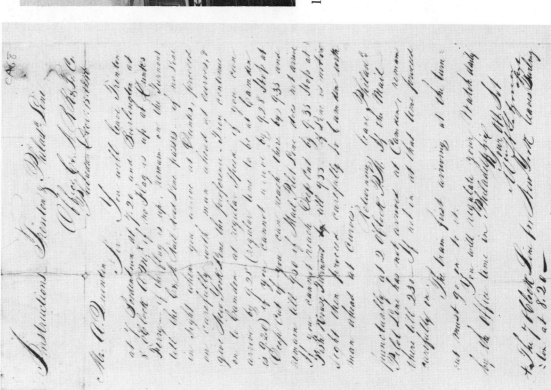

177. Instructions to conductor, Camden & Amboy. 1846—letter by Wm. Gatzmer.

179. Freight cars, Belair, Ohio, 1892.

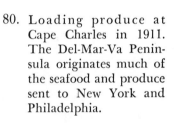

80. Loading produce at Cape Charles in 1911. The Del-Mar-Va Peninsula originates much of the seafood and produce sent to New York and Philadelphia.

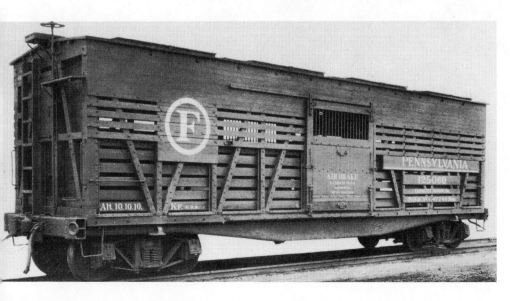

181. S t o c k Car, 1910.

182. Unloading automobile car, early '20's.

183. A special shipment of grain left Chicago at 10:00 A.M. April 30, 1892. Hauled by Pittsburgh, Ft. Wayne & Chicago engine No. 263 all the way to Girard Point, Philadelphia, it consisted of 40 cars and caboose with 66,000 pounds of grain per car. Helper engines were used from Pittsburgh to Derry, Conemaugh to Gallitzin, Columbia to 52nd Street, and over Arsenal Bridge, Philadelphia. Engine class, H3.

184. Container car handling.

185. A car rider at 52nd Street, Philadelphia, on a car going over the "hump." When cars are classified and switched to the proper track, the "rider" sets the brakes. Car retarders in many yards are eliminating this form of braking.

186. Pick-up and delivery service gives freight shippers much of the convenience of express in that railroad trucks are used at both ends of the shipment, eliminating the necessity of hiring local trucks.

187. Altoona Shops as they first appeared in 1852.

188. Altoona Shops, 1869.

189. Interior of Altoona Shops, 1869.

191. Interior of roundhouse at Altoona Shops, 1875.

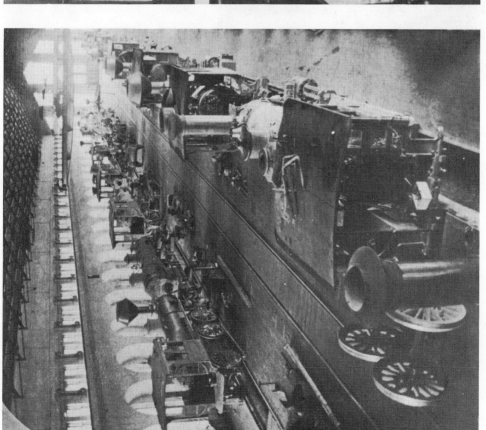

190. Interior of Altoona Shops, 1875.

IN STEAM READY FOR TRIAL.
Tuesday, 2:50 p. m

16 HOURS 50 MINUTES WORK.

WHEELS UNDER AND CAB IN POSITION.
Tuesday, 7 o'clock a. m.

10 HOURS WORK.

BOILER IN POSITION.
Monday, Noon.

5 HOURS WORK.

COMMENCEMENT.
Monday, 7 o'clock a. m.

192. Stages in erecting a locomotive in 16 hours, 50 minutes at the Altoona Shops in 1888.

193. Altoona Shops (Juniata Shop).

194. Fitting a tire to a driving wheel. Expanded by heat, the tire when cool shrinks to a tight fit on the cast wheel.

195. An overhead crane with a class L1 locomotive.

196. Testing plant at the Altoona Shops.

197. Warehouse, Cincinnati, 1892.

98. Indianapolis Car Shops, 1892.

199. Harrisburg roundhouse, 1869.

200. Enola Yard, Harrisburg, largest freight yard in the world.

201. Pitcairn Yard.

202. Greenwich coal piers.

03. Sandusky docks.

204. Ore loaders.

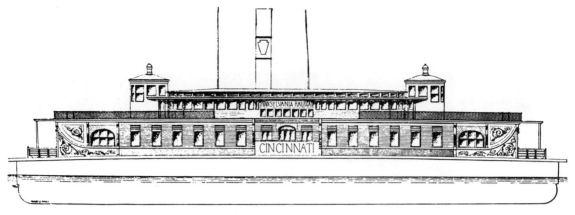

205. Ferryboat, "Cincinnati," 1892

206. Modern Ferry, "Wildwood."

207. Cape Charles passenger and automobile ferry, "Princess Anne."

08. Tug boat and car float.

09. Greenville car float dock.

PART FIVE
LOCOMOTIVE
DEVELOPMENT

Early Engines on Affiliated Lines

FOR THE earliest engine built and used on any railroad which is now incorporated into the Pennsylvania, the Camden and Amboy can be credited. When Robert Stevens made his trip to England in 1830, he was present at the trials of the Stephenson engine "Planet." It appeared so satisfactory that he ordered a similar locomotive for the Camden and Amboy. This engine, known as the "John Bull" or "No. 1," was completed in May 1831, and disassembled and forwarded by the ship *Allegheny* in June. In August it arrived at Philadelphia—from where it was sent by sloop to Bordentown. Isaac Dripps, a young mechanic then employed in repairing the Stevens steamboats on the Delaware, was assigned to put the engine in running order. On its arrival the boiler and cylinders were in place, but the wheels, rods, pistons, valves, etc., were packed in boxes. No drawings came with the parts, and Dripps had to decide its assembly for himself. After several attempts he succeeded in putting it together. No tender came with the engine, and a four-wheeled flatcar was improvised, upon which a whiskey cask served to carry the water supply. This was connected with the engine by a shoe-leather hose made by a local cobbler. On the 12th of November, 1831, members of the legislature and other state officials came to Bordentown to attend the first official trial of the new engine, which made several trips over a short stretch of track with two stage-coach type cars built by the carriage manufacturers M. P. and M. E. Green, of Hoboken. Shortly after this demonstration, Matthias Baldwin came to Bordentown and with Dripps' permission inspected the engine. His own later designs for his model used at Peale's Museum and the "Old Ironsides" reflected some of "John Bull's" features.

One difficulty with the "John Bull" was that it had a tendency for frequently getting off the track. To correct this, Stevens devised an oak frame carrying a 26-inch pair of wheels; this was attached to the ends of the forward main axle. The coupling rods were removed and one of the former wheels made loose on the axle for additional play on curves. The pilot, the first ever designed, was applied in 1832. The cab seen in later photos was a much later addition.

A very interesting early Camden and Amboy locomotive was the "Monster," which, as far as can be ascertained, first ran in 1834. This was a result of collaboration between Robert Stevens and Isaac Dripps; illustration No. 220 shows this unusual design as built, and No. 221 shows it as rebuilt in 1869 and used up to 1875. Weighing more than 30 tons, probably the heaviest engine of its time, it had 48-inch drivers. Three more engines of this type were built by the Trenton Locomotive Works shortly after their establishment in 1853, when Dripps was one of the partners.

The Camden and Amboy had several other peculiar engines as a result of another trip made by Stevens to England in 1845. There he was impressed by the large-drivered Crampton engines, which had a single pair of driving wheels, and upon his return he asked Dripps to design a similar type with 8-foot drivers. The plans were approved in 1847, and the order was given Richard Norris & Son, who delivered No. 48, the first of its kind, in 1849. Dripps decided after watching its performance that a single pair of drivers did not give sufficient adhesion and opposed ordering more engines of this class. He was overruled, however, and several more, some with smaller wheels, were later placed in service. Six cars were about their limit in hauling capacity and even then they had trouble in starting, but once under way they were very fast. They were in use until about 1862, and one, rebuilt as a 4-4-0, was in service until 1865.

William Mason, one of the country's foremost early locomotive builders, made his first engine for the Jeffersonville Railroad in 1843. This was the "James Guthrie," named for one of the directors of the Road; it was followed a month later by the "William G. Armstrong," named for its president. The two engines were similar in design; the first had 66-inch drivers and the second 72-inch drivers, and each weighed 30 tons. Reuben Wells, then Master Mechanic of the Road, later said they "were extremely neat and well finished — more so probably than any engines turned out by other builders at that period. Taking these engines altogether, they may in most respects be said to have been a little 'ahead of the times' in design, finish and general proportions."

For use on the Madison inclined plane, the Madison & Indianapolis Railroad placed in service in 1846-47 the Baldwin-built "M. G. Bright." Illustration No. 217 shows this engine as rebuilt some twenty years later. Originally, besides the conventional cylinder and drive, it had a pair of vertical cylinders above the boiler. The connecting rods worked by these cylinders operated a shaft under the boiler which carried a cog wheel; this engaged another twice as large which, in turn, worked in a rack rail in the center of the track. The shaft carrying the large cog could be raised or lowered by means of connecting rods and a lever operated by a small horizontal cylinder on top of the boiler. Thus the engine could be operated as any other by adhesion only, or, when it was on the inclined plane, the cogwheel could be lowered into the rack and extra power obtained with the additional cylinders. Another locomotive of this type, the "John Brough," was built by Baldwin in 1850. Its drivers were 42 inches in diameter.

In 1858, the "Reuben Wells," named after its designer, was built especially for use on the plane, and it is supposed to be the first engine to climb a grade of 310 feet to the mile (illustration No. 246). It had 44-inch drivers and 20- by 24-inch cylinders, and weighed 112,000 pounds. 1,800 gallons of water were carried in the cylindrical tanks on either side. It was used regularly for twenty-eight years and then in partial service for ten years more. It is now preserved at Purdue University. A lighter engine of the same type, the "W. J. Bright," followed it.

The first locomotives to be used on the Philadelphia & Columbia were built by Norris—the "Green Hawk," which was not very successful, the "Black Hawk"—improved somewhat—and an unnamed engine unofficially called the "Tomahawk." Two English locomotives are also mentioned in early reference to this line's motive power, but the first really successful engine was Baldwin's "Lancaster," which was followed by the "Columbia"—both these and some twenty-five others following, until 1842, being of the same 4-2-0 type.

On July 10, 1836, a most unusual event occurred on the Belmont inclined plane, when William Norris' locomotive, the four-and-a-half-ton "George Washington," hauled a load of 19,200 pounds up this grade at a speed of 15 miles an hour. This was the first locomotive to climb such a grade, and so remarkable was the feat that current reports in engineering papers were, despite verification, generally disbelieved. A second trial on July 19 proved the engine's capabilities. The wheel arrangement was similar to that of the Baldwin engines, except that the driving wheels were placed forward of the firebox, thus providing more adhesion. The Baldwin locomotives with their longer wheel bases were steadier riders and were generally used for passenger service, while those of Norris were preferred for freight. Illustration No. 215 is reasonably accurate, although there is some conflicting evidence to the effect that the "George Washington" was an "inside-connected" engine—meaning that it may have had a cranked driving axle with the rods and cylinders inside the frames.

The "Boston," first locomotive to be used on the Portage Railroad, was put in service in May 1835. Its weight was 8½ tons, and its driving wheels were 4 feet in diameter. Other engines following were the "Delaware," "Allegheny," and "Pittsburgh," whose wheel arrangements were generally similar to those of the Philadelphia & Columbia engines.

When the Pennsylvania took over the State System in 1857, it acquired 70 to 75 locomotives. Thereafter it numbered its locomotives rather than naming them as before. Some of the state engines had very picturesque names, such as "Old Fogy," "Fingall's Baby," "Corporal Trimm," "My Son Samuel," and "Tam O'Shanter."

The Baltimore & Susquehanna's first locomotive was the Stephenson-built "Herald," which was placed in service in the early '30's. That on the Philadelphia & Trenton was the "Black Hawk," a Baldwin engine of 1835.

Pennsylvania Railroad Locomotives to 1867

According to available information, the first locomotives to be built for the Pennsylvania, the "Dauphin" and the "Perry," were supplied by the Baldwin Locomotive Works. These were completed by Baldwin in November 1848, before the opening of the road. They were of the 0-8-0 type, with Baldwin flexible beam trucks. Some years later they were sold to the Philadelphia & Reading Railroad. A third of similar design, the "Westmoreland," built early in 1850, continued in service on the Pennsylvania until 1866, later becoming No. 14.

Although delivered earlier, these engines were not the first to be placed in actual service on the line. The first locomotive built for the Pennsylvania and placed in service was the "Mifflin," a fast passenger locomotive, built by Baldwin, in July 1849. Two locomotives of the same type, the "Blair" and the "Indiana," came in January 1850. They averaged 4,700 pounds in weight, had cylinders 14 inches by 20 inches, drivers 72 inches in diameter, "carrying" wheels 46 inches in diameter, and truck wheels 33 inches in diameter.

These engines, known as the Crampton type, had a single pair of drivers and "carrying wheels" which were placed in front of the fire box. A lever from the cab was connected to equalizers so that when starting, weight could be thrown off the carrying wheels upon the drivers and returned when sufficient headway had been obtained. The total weight was 47,000 pounds, of which the drivers carried 18,000 pounds, the carrying wheels 14,000 pounds, and the trucks 15,000 pounds. The use of the lever increased the weight on the drivers to 24,000 pounds, while of course reducing that on the carrying wheels. The tenders of these engines held about 1,300 gallons of water. These locomotives were built for speed; one had a record of four miles in three minutes and another a fairly long run at a speed of a mile a minute.

Several Baldwin locomotives of the 4-4-0 type built during the years 1849 and 1852 were examples of the type of motive power widely used at that time for most passenger and freight service. Among these were the "Juniata" and the "Huntington," built in 1849 and having 14- to 20-inch cylinders and 54-inch drivers. In 1850 the "Allegheny" and the "Clarion" (see illustration No. 222), having 14½- by 20-inch cylinders and 54-inch drivers, were placed in service. The "Clinton," the "Columbia," the "Elk," the "Erie," the "Venango," and the "Centre," of the same type, with cylinders 15 by 20 inches and 54-inch drivers, were also built in 1850, as were two other pairs of locomotives, the "Wyoming" and the "Armstrong," with 13½- by 22-inch cylinders and 60-inch drivers (4-4-0 type). The other class was of the 0-8-0 type, the "Westmoreland" having 17- by 22-inch cylinders and 43-inch drivers, and the "Beaver" with 14½- by 18-inch cylinders and 42-inch drivers, these being the same type as the "Perry."

In 1851 the "Clearfield," the "Crawford," and the "Bradford," and possibly another were built by Baldwin. They were of the 4-4-0 type with 15- by 20-inch cylinders and 54-inch drivers. In 1852 two locomotives of the same type as the "Juniata," named the "Fayette" and the "Green," having 15- by 20-inch cylinders and 54-inch drivers, were built by Baldwin. Other engines supplied this year by Baldwin were the "Butler" (later rebuilt and known as No. 26) and the "Susquehanna," with 13½- by 22-inch cylinders, and three others, the "Somerset," the "Pike," and the "Union," with cylinders 15 by 20 inches.

At the beginning of 1852 President Thompson ordered certain types of engines from Baldwin and Smith & Perkins for handling trains over the main line grades. An approximate weight was specified and either a two- or four-wheel leading truck could be used. Twelve locomotives were built by each firm, and deliveries were made between August and the end of the year, one of the Baldwin engines, the "Berks," going to the Philadelphia & Columbia Railroad. All were six-coupled, and six, the "Bradford," the "Dauphin," the "Lawrence," the "Mercer," the "Lebanon," and the "Berks," were built with four-wheel lead trucks, 18-by 22-inch cylinders, and 44-inch drivers. They weighed approximately 64,500 pounds, with 46,000 pounds on the drivers. The other six had a pair of leading wheels placed directly under the cylinders. This type probably weighed about 60,000 pounds with 48,000 pounds on the drivers. It is possible, however, that some carried as much as 18,000 or 19,000 pounds on the leading wheels, which at that time was considered excessive. Therefore, these six locomotives, one of which was the "Cumberland," were later rebuilt by the Pennsylvania, with four-wheel trucks replacing the original single pair of leading wheels.

The locomotives built by Smith & Perkins were of the same type as Millholland's Philadelphia & Reading design. They were six-coupled engines with a pair of carrying wheels behind the cylinders. It was found that the use of the small wheels forward of the drivers was necessary to prevent flange cutting on curves. This wheel arrangement was the forerunner of the experiments leading to the Mogul type, designed some ten years later. These engines had cylinders 17 by 22 inches in diameter, and the weight of the locomotives was 54,000 pounds. The boilers were straight, but two of the group, of which one was the "Latrobe," had "Wagon Top" boilers which were then in the experimental stage.

Besides the Baldwin and Smith & Perkins engines of the 2-6-0 type, the records show that two Richard Norris & Sons engines of the same type were delivered to the state road during the years 1852 and 1854 and were acquired by the Pennsylvania in 1857. Two Norris engines built in February and March 1854 and used for freight service on the Pennsylvania Railroad were the "Kittatinny" and "Allegrippus." When numbers were assigned in the place of names in 1857, the former became No. 92 and the latter No. 96. During the same month that it was placed in service, the "Allegrippus" was in an accident that was probably the first on record and of any importance in the Alleghenies after the opening of the present main line. About three miles above the Horseshoe Curve, the recently finished embankment gave way and the engine fell forty feet down the hillside. Thomas Ridley, the engineer, was badly injured, and he always thereafter referred to the location of the accident as "Allegrippus." Some years later, when the company built a station at this point, it was called Allegrippus. It is still known by this name.

From 1853 to 1856 eleven "Camel" type locomotives were completed by Ross Winans of Baltimore for the Pennsylvania. These locomotives had 19- by 22-inch cylinders and 44-inch drivers and averaged 59,000 pounds in total weight. They were typical Winans engines with long overhanging fire boxes, firing chutes, chain-operated valve gear, and other unusual features. The first of these locomotives was considerably rebuilt shortly after it was delivered to the Pennsylvania, and five were rebuilt without the firing chutes and with the fire boxes closed at the rear. All were later rebuilt as Moguls (2-6-0) at Altoona, and as such some were in service until 1880 to 1882.

Most of the Norris locomotives coming to the Pennsylvania in the early '50's were of the American (4-4-0) type. In 1853 twelve were built for passenger service, three having 72-inch drivers. In 1853 and 1854 eight more with 54-inch drivers were built for freight service. The Norris locomotives were well known for speed; but some parts, especially the frames, were not heavy enough, and some of the boilers were so poorly stayed that explosions often occurred. Among the nine Norris engines with 60-inch drivers was one called the "Loyalhanna."

In 1852 the Laird type of crosshead was first tried. Some years later, in 1857, they were extensively applied to most Pennsylvania locomotives. At this time the cost of engines, according to the Baldwin records, was $6,750 for 18-ton and $7,100 for 20-ton engines.

The Baldwin variable cutoff was used on a considerable number of Pennsylvania locomotives for passenger and freight service. Among these were two fast passenger engines with 72-inch drivers delivered late in 1854, and named the "Belle" and the "Flirt." The general design of these locomotives was representative of the 4-4-0 type then built by

Baldwin for both passenger and freight service. Freight locomotives of the o-8-o type built during the years 1854 and 1856 also had the variable cutoff.

In 1856 two improved Norris locomotives with 16- by 24-inch cylinders and 66-inch drivers were put into operation on the Pennsylvania. The engines had the Stephenson shifting link motion, being probably the first Norris engines to use this.

American motive power officials generally had been coming to favor the link motion, and Baldwin had used it at times when it was specified on locomotive orders. The first Baldwin locomotive for the Pennsylvania in which this was used was the "Tiger," a 4-4-0 type for the fast passenger service delivered in December 1856. The "Leopard," the "Hornet," and the "Wasp," of this same type, arrived a short time later. These engines had straight boilers with two domes; in this design a form of construction was begun which was often followed until 1880. The "Tiger" was elegantly painted and embellished after the practice of the day, and at that time it represented the ultimate in the American passenger locomotive design.

The development of the link motion was an outstanding milestone in locomotive development. The most advanced engines of the late '50's and the '60's embodied many of the outstanding features of the locomotive as built for several decades following. During the next ten or twelve years the locomotives built for the Pennsylvania's main line service were largely of two types—the American (4-4-0) for passenger service and fast freight, and the ten-wheel (4-6-0) for heavy freight. These two types, although no longer used for this heaviest kind of work, were still represented in the motive power roster of the road by a number of excellent locomotives built after 1900.

When the Pennsylvania Railroad first began operating, wood was used everywhere as locomotive fuel, although some experiments had been made with coke, and anthracite was being used with varying success on several roads. In 1853 a series of experiments with wood, coke, and Pittsburgh and Allegheny coals was made in order to determine which fuel would be most economical and satisfactory. The results indicated that coal would prove best, especially when mixed with wood.

Much more exhaustive tests were run in 1859 for five months to determine whether it would be practical to use bituminous coal in passenger service without creating objectionable smoke. All the passenger locomotives on the road were then burning wood. Six locomotives were used in these tests, three of which definitely proved that it was possible to use bituminous coal in passenger service if the boilers of the locomotives had ample combustion chambers with means for adequately baffling and mixing gases.

A series of tests was later made with Engine No. 156, a new Baldwin 4-4-0 type, with what was known as the Smith boiler, designed especially for burning coal. The test was run to determine the relative heating value of a ton of coal and a cord of wood, as well as the relative costs of fuels and engine repairs due to the substitution of coal for wood. The results indicated that as a basis of calculation, one pound of Pittsburgh coal was equivalent in heating value to 2.31 pounds of wood, and that one net ton of coal was equal to $1\frac{1}{3}$ cords of hard wood. The relative cost of coal and wood as fuel was determined for the different divisions of the road and the feasibility of burning coal in passenger service was fully demonstrated.

In the experiments to determine methods of burning bituminous coal successfully, unusual boilers such as the Dimpfel and Phleger were designed and tried and experiments were made with a considerable variety of combustion chambers, baffle plates, and similar devices. Four ten-wheeled engines of the Phleger type were built for the Pennsylvania Railroad between 1857 and 1862 by R. Norris and Son. The Pennsylvania was responsible for much of the progress made in determining the value of such devices, and experience fully demonstrated that success in burning coal depended as much upon the fireman as upon the special equipment used on the locomotive. The value of the fire brick arch, especially when high volatile coal is used, was proved in these tests, and this feature is today generally recognized as an essential part of any coal-burning locomotive.

The first locomotive to use an injector instead of a water pump was built by Baldwin early in 1861 (their construction No. 1000). It bore the road number 212 and the name "M. W. Baldwin." It was a light passenger locomotive of the 2-4-0 type, with 10- by 18-inch cylinders and 56-inch drivers. Two more engines similar, but with four-wheel trucks, were built later.

John P. Laird was appointed Master of Machinery in June 1862, retaining this position until May 1866. He was a particularly capable engineer and his ideas were reflected in much of the design and development of Pennsylvania motive power. Among his notable contributions were a balloon stack which proved a great success as a spark arrester on coal-burning locomotives and a type of two-bar guide which now bears his name and is still frequently used in modified form on heavy locomotives. Laird was also responsible for rebuilding and improving many of the old locomotives and, as far as possible, he attempted to standardize the many types and designs then on the road. This was the result of the Pennsylvania's acquiring the State Sysytem in 1857.

The standard passenger locomotive in the '60's was of the American (4-4-0) type with "spread" truck wheels, horizontal cylinders, plain slide valves, Stephenson link motion, and a wagon-top boiler having a deep firebox between the driving axles. The freight locomotive of the ten-wheel (4-6-0) type was in many respects similar. The largest passenger locomotives had 17- by 24-inch cylinders and drivers from 60 to 66 inches in diameter, while the heavy ten-wheelers for freight service had 18- by 22-inch cylinders and 54-inch drivers. Injectors were occasionally substituted for pumps. The need for a brake more efficient than the ordinary hand brake, especially in passenger service, was becoming evident. The Loughridge chain brake was used extensively on the Pennsylvania and was at the time the best system yet devised. It consisted of a friction wheel which could be drawn against the rear driving wheel of the locomotive. As this rotated, a chain was wound up on its shaft and the pull of this chain was transmitted to the brake shoes throughout the train.

In the '60's, too, steel was used more and more in locomotive construction, and the Pennsylvania was a pioneer in using this material. Steel fire-boxes were first made by Baldwin for the Pennsylvania in 1861. High-temper English steel was used, but the plates cracked when being fitted to the boilers and it was necessary to replace them with copper ones. American homogeneous cast steel was successfully used for the fireboxes of engines Nos. 231 and 232 in January 1862. These were ten-wheel freight locomotives and the inside fireboxes and combustion chambers, 36 inches deep; with the exception of the tube sheets, which were copper, were built of steel plates throughout. Steel boiler shells were first supplied by Baldwin for the Pennsylvania in 1868, and the first steel boiler tubes were used in three ten-wheelers built by Baldwin.

In 1862 the last of the wood-burning freight engines were withdrawn from service.

The first four-wheel swing-bolster truck was that used on an American-type locomotive built by Baldwin for the Pennsylvania in 1867. Four fast passenger engines using this truck and having 17- by 24-inch cylinders and 66-inch drivers, were numbered 419 to 422. Engine No. 422 was placed in service September 9, 1867, and until May 14, 1871, was con-tinually in service without being off its wheels for repairs, covering in this period 153,280 miles.

Standardization and Designs of Locomotives to 1900

On November 16, 1867, Alexander J. Cassatt became Master of Ma chinery, and under his direction a start was made toward the standardiz-ing of motor power, this need having been evident for some time. The first group of "standard" locomotives, placed in service between 1868 and 1872, consisted of eight classes of engines wherein interchangeable parts and details were used as far as possible.

LOCOMOTIVE CLASSIFICATION 1867-1895

In 1867 three classes, "A," "B," and "C," were established and others added as in the list below.

Class	Date Established	Wheels Driver	Trucks	Diam. Driver in inches	Cylinder in inches	Pressure lbs.	Service
A	1867	4	4	68	17 x 24	125	Pass. light traffic
B	1867	4	4	62	18 x 24	125	Pass. mountain helpers
C	1867	4	4	62	17 x 24	125	Pass. & fast freight
D	1868	6	4	56	18 x 22	125	Freight for general service
E	1869	6	4	50	18 x 22	125	Freight—heavy mountain service
F	1869	6	0	44	15 x 18	125	Shifting—saddle tanks
G	1870	4	4	56	15 x 22	125	Pass. light service on branches
H	1872	6	0	44	15 x 22	125	Shifting—separate tender
C An-thracite	1873	4	4	62	17 x 24	125	Pass.—anthracite coal
I	1875	8	2	50	20 x 24	125	Freight—mt. traffic & heavy trains
K	1880	4	4	78	18 x 24	140	Pass. especially for express service
B—a	1881	4	4	68	18 x 24	125	Pass.
L (First L)	1881	4	4	only one built			Pass.—heavy express train
L	1895	4	4	68 & 80	18½ x 26	185	Pass.—heavy express train
A An-thracite	1882	4	4	68	17 x 24	140	Pass. anthracite coal, light service
M	1882	6	0	50	19 x 24	125	Shifting—heavy service full trains
N	1883	4	4	62	17 x 24	130	Pass., large boiler replacing Class "C"
O	1883	4	4	62	18 x 24	130	Pass. similar to "N" but larger cylinders
P	1883	4	4	62	18½ x 24	140	Pass. general service
Q	1885	4	0	44	15 x 22	125	Shifting—light service at warehouses
R	1885	8	2	50	20 x 24	140	Freight, consolidation replacing Class "I"
S	1887	8	2	50	20 x 24	140	Freight, consolidation lighter than "R"
T	1892	4	4	84	H.P. 19½ x 28 L.P. 31 x 28	50%	Pass. compound
X	1893	6	4	68	19 x 24	180	Pass. exp. service with heavy train
U	1893	4	0	50	17 x 24	160	Shifting—heavy service

According to annual reports, some early totals of locomotives are as follows:

December 31, 1855	118 locomotives
December 31, 1862	255 locomotives
December 31, 1863	290 locomotives
December 31, 1864	321 locomotives
December 31, 1865	352 locomotives
December 31, 1866	362 locomotives
December 31, 1867	428 locomotives
December 31, 1868	434 locomotives
December 31, 1869	477 locomotives
December 31, 1871	514 locomotives (Including 88 in shops, 126 on Phila. & Erie)
December 31, 1872	916 locomotives (563 on Pennsylvania Railroad)
December 31, 1873	1,071 locomotives (662 on Pennsylvania Railroad, 259 on United Railroads of N. J., 150 on Philadelphia & Erie)
December 31, 1874	1,075 locomotives
December 31, 1895	1,803 locomotives (1,187 on Pennsylvania Railroad, 409 on United Railroads of N. J., 207 on Philadelphia & Erie)

In April 1869 the first experimental trial of air brakes was made on the Pan Handle Division. Patented by George Westinghouse, the installation was on the Steubenville accommodation, which made daily an 86-mile round trip between that town and Pittsburgh. This was undoubtedly the first train in the world to be so controlled, and the officers of the Pennsylvania watched the trials for several months. In September this device was installed on engine No. 360 of the Pittsburgh Division, but as some improvements were necessary, it was removed, rebuilt, and put on locomotive No. 45. Six passenger cars were equipped with air cylinders, levers, and brakes, and in November the first train with air brakes ran from Pittsburgh to Altoona. So successful were the demonstrations that other railroads immediately became interested, and from that point on the air brake's development and installation was rapid. All passenger locomotives on the Pennsylvania had automatic air brakes by July 1, 1879, and it was the first railroad to adopt them as standard.

The first Baldwin-built engine following the standard classification plan was No. 154, delivered in July 1868, a Class D (G1) and the first of

255 bituminous engines of this type built between 1868 and 1873. The first Class I (H1) locomotive was built at Altoona in 1875 and later that year fourteen more were ordered from Baldwin's. Class C standard 4-4-0 locomotives were built and used in passenger service more extensively than any other, and they made long nonstop runs because of being able to take water from track tanks.

On April 10, 1876, a general order was issued providing for the first "pooling" of locomotives. In 1878 the first automatic bell ringers were installed on locomotives.

In March 1881 ten passenger locomotives known as Class K were put in service, hauling trains between New York and Philadelphia (90 miles) in 110 minutes. They had 78-inch drivers, and had wagon-top boilers on top of the main frames. These were the first engines with a high center of gravity as well as the first to have the boiler pressure increased from 125 to 140 pounds. They were the first to use steam reversing gear. So successful were these engines that the following year the Class A anthracite (D7) was designed, having 17- by 24-inch cylinders and 68-inch drivers. The N, O, and P classes were also designed in 1883, as was a heavy switcher Class M (B3). The P class had 18½ by 24-inch cylinders and 68-inch drivers and was used for heavy passenger service on New York and other divisions. It was similar to Class K, but had 21 per cent more tractive force with only 4 per cent increase of weight.

Twenty-five notable consolidation-type engines were built at Altoona in 1886, the first with Belpaire-type fireboxes and known as Class R (H3). These also had 140-pound boiler pressure. They were highly successful and were subsequently built in large numbers and widely used everywhere on the system.

In 1887 a locomotive was fitted with an oil-burning device for testing the efficiency of oil firing, and it was found that one pound of petroleum properly burned equaled 1¾ pounds of coal in generating steam. However, at that time the Pennsylvania Railroad used about 8,000 tons of coal daily, and if oil could have been substituted it would have required over one-third of that year's total production of oil in the United States.

It was estimated that refineries would have increased the price of oil so that it could not be burned in competition with coal, and this was the deciding factor which prevented the change to oil.

In 1888 the feat of assembling a locomotive in the short time of 16 hours and 50 minutes was demonstrated (illustration No. 192). The *Railroad Gazette* in reporting the story says:

> When the work commences in the erecting shop the engine is in the state shown in our lowest illustration. The frames are completely finished, all the cross-bars have been attached and the cylinders mounted on the frames in the frame shop. The cylinders and guides are completely lined up in the same shop, so when the structure arrives in the locomotive erecting shop, all that remains to be done is to put the cross-heads into the guides, put the pistons into the cylinders and key the piston in the cross-head. No adjustment whatever of guides or cross-heads is made in the locomotive erecting shop.
>
> The boiler was then brought in, most of the fittings and tubes having been previously attached, and, generally speaking, the 16 hours and 50 minutes' work represented the time required for the assembling of the parts, erecting the locomotive, and attaching such parts as are necessary in putting the different parts together.
>
> The time, 16 hours and 50 minutes, is believed to be the quickest time in which anything of this kind was ever done, the best previous record being about 24 hours.

In 1895 a new American type of locomotive, the Class L, with 68- and 80-inch drivers, was built to haul heavy trains at high speed. They had 185 pounds pressure, weighed 135,000 pounds (the heaviest so far built), and represented the most advanced practice to date. Class L with 68-inch drivers was reclassified as D16, and the L engines with 80-inch driving wheels became Class D16a.

The first passenger engines to have the Belpaire firebox were the Classes O and P (D9, D10, and D12), this being substituted in 1889. Several experimental 4-4-0 locomotives were built in 1892 as the need for heavier power was becoming evident. Six Class P (D14) engines with 78-inch diameter drivers instead of 68 inches were built at Altoona in 1893. A number of changes were again made in this class the following year, resulting in Class D14a.

Ten-wheel engines were first built at the Fort Wayne Shops in 1893, being old Class X (G3), and in 1899 others (G4) were built at Altoona, followed by the Baldwin-built G4a type in 1900.

More powerful freight engines than the Class R (H3) were becoming necessary in 1895, and the F1 and F1a Mogul (2-6-0) type were designed. In 1898 the first H5 (2-8-0) was tried. The following is a contemporary report from *Locomotive Engineering* for June 1898:

> The Pennsylvania Railroad Company's new Class H5 Locomotive, No. 872, was recently turned out of the Juniata Shops, at Altoona. While it has been in service but a few days, it is showing evidence of splendid working ability.
>
> In the preliminary tests made on the Pittsburgh division, it was found that the H5 could handle 568 tons light, and 643 tons loaded. The record of the standard Class R freight engine is 350 tons light and 383 tons loaded, and for the Mogul, 375 tons light and 433 tons loaded. It will be seen from this that the Class H5 will eclipse any other locomotive on the Pennsylvania system.
>
> The engine is too big to be turned on any of the Altoona turntables, and she therefore is used as a helper above Altoona, backing down the mountain.

Twentieth-Century Locomotives

Atlantic or 4-4-2 locomotives had for several years before 1900 been proving themselves generally very successful in high-speed passenger work. So in 1899 three were built by the Pennsylania at Altoona, becoming Class E1 for use between Camden and Atlantic City. In this service they performed very satisfactorily, hauling 300-ton trains at 75 miles per hour. These engines had 80-inch drivers and a total weight of about 86 tons. They were the only Pennsylvania engines to have the cab in the center of the boiler. Following this class were other Atlantics of Class E1a, E2, and E3, with radial stayed fireboxes. The later E2a and E3a had Belpaire fireboxes. These engines were designed while W. W. Atterbury was General Superintendent of Motive Power, from October 1901 to January 1903. Atlantics became practically the standard for fast passenger service for more than 10 years.

The H6 Consolidation engines were improved by wide fireboxes in 1901, when two H6a types were built by Baldwin's. As a result, more than a thousand were ordered from Baldwin's between 1902 and 1905. Many were also built at Altoona. After experiments, ten of these had Walschaerts valve gear applied, and as it soon proved itself in easier maintenance, it began to be used generally. Mogul types F1, F3, F3B, and finally F3c with a Belpaire firebox were also being built for fast freight service, some 163 of which were Baldwin. They were put in service from 1901 to 1903.

The Walschaerts valve gear having been so satisfactory, it was used on later Atlantics in 1906—Classes E2d and E3d. About this time the increasing weight of passenger equipment led to an experimental Pacific (4-6-2) type ordered from the American Locomotive Company (illustration No. 266), and as a result the K2 was designed at Fort Wayne in 1910 and a large number were built at Altoona. The K2 engine No. 7514 was the first on the Pennsylvania to use superheated steam, an innovation introduced in 1911. This was so important an improvement that superheaters became standard for all Pennsylvania locomotives in 1913. In this year 30 engines of the K3s class, generally the same as K2 but with superheaters, were built by Baldwin's.

In 1910 still more powerful freight motive power began to be needed. The answer to this need was the H8 type, larger than the H6s and with 62-inch drivers, followed by the H9s and H10s in 1913, some of the latter with automatic stokers.

In 1910 the heaviest Atlantic, the E6, was designed, and tests the following year showed it to be generally better than the K2. Two other experimental engines followed, and in 1913, 80 of Class E6s were built at Altoona and were placed in service handling the heaviest fast passenger trains on the New York and New Jersey divisions.

Still heavier power was required to handle passenger trains through the mountains, and a new Pacific, the K4s, was designed and built at Altoona in 1914, using many features of the E6s. These became the standard passenger engine of the Pennsylvania, being built in large numbers, only minor improvements being added through the next fifteen years.

The Mikado, a 2-8-2 type (L1s) was designed about the same time. It has the same boiler as the K4 and about a 25 per cent increase in tractive force over the H9s.

Switching engines were, through the years mentioned, also being considerably improved. An 85-ton switcher (B6) was built first in 1902. From this evolved the B6sb, a much improved 0-6-0 type which, built first in 1913, has become the standard of this wheel arrangement. Some lighter engines, Class B8, were also built from 1903 to 1905 and 1906, 62 being supplied by Baldwin's. For lighter work the A4, an 0-4-0 type, was designed in 1904, followed in 1916 by the A5s, which weighs nearly 66 tons. Latest of steam switchers was the C1 Class (0-8-0) first designed in 1924.

The first Decapod (I1s) was an experimental one built at Altoona in 1916 and tried in heavy freight service. As a result of its tests, 123 Juniata-built engines followed, and later, in 1922 and 1923, 475 more came from Baldwin's. These engines had mechanical stokers and feed water heaters and have been, until fairly recently, the standard for heavy freight service.

Sixty engines of the N1s (2-10-2) type were built by Baldwin's and American Locomotive Co. in 1918 and 1919 and were among the most powerful of this wheel arrangement built. Their tractive force was 84,800 pounds and their weight nearly 240 tons. Thirty engines of the N2s, the standard United States Railroad Administration design, were built by Baldwin's and used on lines west of Pittsburgh.

Some experimental Mallet articulated engines have been used on the Pennsylvania, one of the 0-8-8-0 and another of the 2-8-8-2 type in 1912. In 1919 Baldwin's built ten compound engines of the 0-8-8-0 type for pushing and heavy yard service, and the same year the most powerful single expansion engine, designed by the Pennsylvania, was built at Altoona. This was the HC1s, a 2-8-8-0 type (illustration No. 272), which could develop a tractive force of 135,000 pounds. It was used experimentally, mostly in pusher service, because its draw bar pull was too great for most couplers at the time.

The Mountain type (4-8-2) Class M1 was built in 1923 for heavy passenger or fast freight service, having a tractive force of 64,550 pounds and steam pressure of 250 pounds and weighing over 191 tons. Two hundred of these engines were built in 1926. In 1923, too, the G5s (4-6-0) was developed principally for suburban service, 90 being built by 1924. The M1a was designed some years later and with its larger tender and improvements over the M1, such as feedwater heaters, was and still is used in either passenger or freight service, where the K4s is too light. In 1930 100 of these engines were placed in service.

In 1936 one of the conventional K4s locomotives underwent a major operation. Streamlined by Raymond Loewy in collaboration with the Pennsylvania Engineering Department, the 3768 forecast a new trend in external design. This was arrived at largely by wind tunnel tests with clay models. Another treatment of streamlining for the K4s is shown in illustration No. 275.

First of the modern multiple-cylindered locomotives was the S1, exhibited under steam on a special treadmill arrangement at the New York World's Fair in 1939. This, the world's largest and fastest coal-burning engine, is 140 feet long, has 84-inch driving wheels, and a tractive force of 71,900 pounds. Built at Altoona, this locomotive is numbered 6100 and was designed to handle 1200 tons on the level at 100 miles per hour.

Several modern freight types are illustrated. The J1 class with a 2-10-4 wheel arrangement and booster are the first in many years not having Belpaire fireboxes, a large number being acquired during World War II.

From the Q1, a four-cylindered 4-6-4-4 type, has come, after redesign-ing, the Q2, of which class 26 are now in service. It can handle a 125-car loaded freight train at speeds better than 50 miles per hour. It was de-veloped to convert more power at speeds over 20 miles per hour than any steam locomotive ever built.

Latest of the four-cylindered fleet are the T1 type, the first order of 50 units in 1945 being divided between Baldwin's and the Altoona Shops. This followed the satisfactory performance of two previously tried which were capable of handling the heaviest passenger trains at speeds up to 100 miles per hour. They are also used in fast freight service.

In 1944, the first coal-burning steam locomotive without cylinders was placed in service on the Pennsylvania. This is the fundamentally differ-ent S2—the first direct-drive steam turbine engine ever made in the United States. Built at Baldwin's, it was jointly designed by Baldwin, Westinghouse, and Pennsylvania engineers. Some of the aims in develop-ing this type of motive power are: eliminating the reciprocating parts of the conventional steam engine, obtaining a uniform application of power to the driving wheels, and gaining the economies that go with turbine drive. The forward turbine develops 6,900 horsepower and the reverse develops 1,500 horsepower. Speeds of 100 miles per hour with a full-length passenger train are easily possible.

Diesel switchers have been used on the Pennsylvania for a number of years. Now, to supplement the steam locomotive over the mountain grades and on unelectrified divisions, main-line road Diesels are being placed in passenger service. Each type of motive power—steam, electric, and Diesel—has its place, and the Pennsylvania does not hesitate to apply each where it can serve most efficiently. In fact, its early anticipation of future needs in every department has become a tradition. In this case, however, the increasing use of Diesels does not mean substitution for steam generally, but merely the improvement of train operation wher-ever possible and wherever necessary.

NOTE: Pennsylvania Railroad motive power as of July 1, 1947, is listed on page 244.

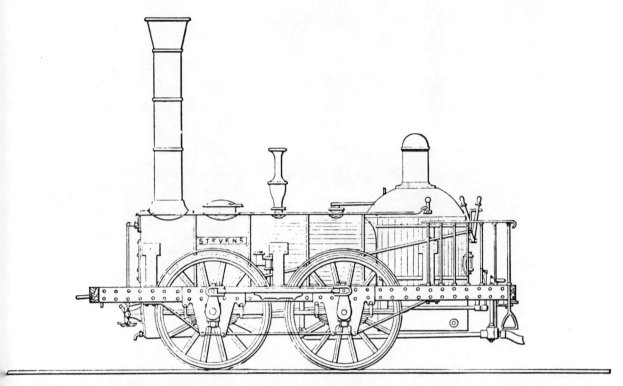

212. "John Bull" as originally built, Camden & Amboy R.R.

213. "John Bull" as rebuilt and now preserved.

214. "Black Hawk," 1835, Philadelphia & Trenton R.R.

215. "Washington," 1836, Philadelphia & Columbia R.R.

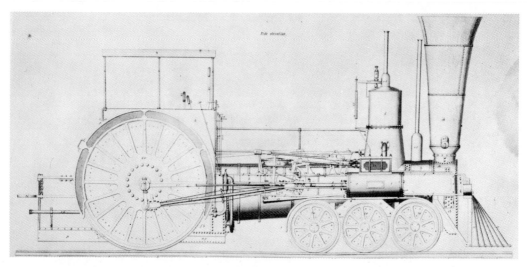

216. "John Stevens," 1849, Camden & Amboy R.R.

217. "M. G. Bright," 1847, Madison & Indianapolis R.R., as rebuilt; photograph probably taken in the '60's.

218. "James Guthrie," 1843, Jeffersonville R.R.

219. "John C. Breckenridge," 1857, Philadelphia & Columbia R.R.

220. "Monster," as built, 1834, Camden & Amboy.

221. "Monster," as rebuilt, 1869.

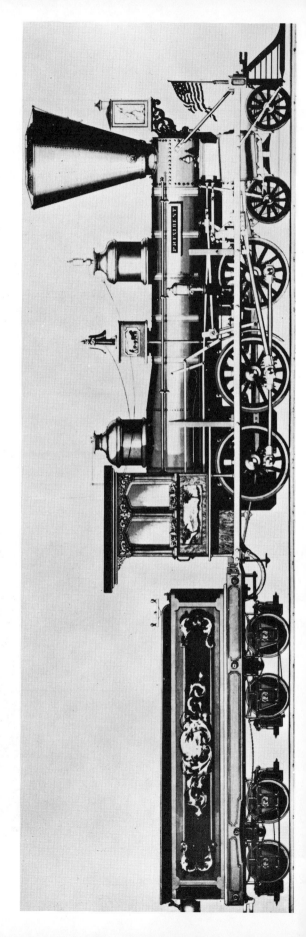

222. "Clarion," built by M. W. Baldwin, 1850.

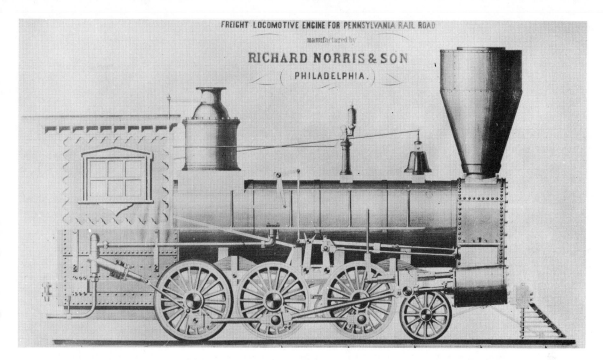

224. "Allegrippus," built by R. Norris & Son, 1854.

25. "Wyoming," built by M. W. Baldwin, 1850.

26. "Antelope," built by Seth Wilmarth, 1852.

227. "Berks," built by M. W. Baldwin, 1852.

228. "Westmoreland," built by Altoona Shops, 1850, later numbered 14.

229. Second No. 14, a Millholland design, built by Norris Works, 1866.

230. No. 40, formerly "Atalanta," built by Seth Wilmarth, 1852.

231. No. 187, formerly "Corporal Trim," built by N. J. Loco. & Mach. Works, 1856.

232. No. 111, taken about 1880.

233. No. 217 as rebuilt 1862, originally Baldwin, 1851.

234. No. 131, "Seneca," as rebuilt 1862, originally (0-8-0) Ross Winans, 1856.

235. No. 214, built by M. W. Baldwin, 1861.

236. No. 45, as rebuilt 1864, formerly "Northumberland," built by M. W. Baldwin, 1853.

237. No. 143, built by M. W. Baldwin, 1862.

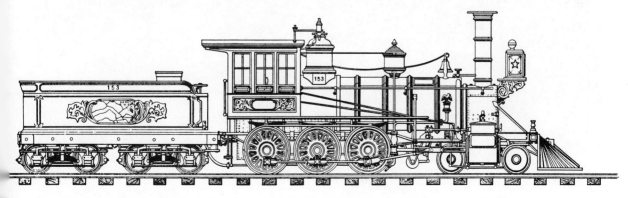

238. No. 153, built by R. Norris & Son, between 1857 and 1862, with Phleger type boiler.

239. No. 3, Bellefonte & Snowshoe Railroad, built by M. W. Baldwin, 1865.

240. A 4-4-0 type on the Little Miami Railroad in the '60's.

41. "Jenny Lind," an early Cumberland Valley engine.

42. Another engine with a single pair of drivers on the Cumberland Valley.

243. No. 7, New Jersey Railroad & Transportation Co., 1867.

244. "John Lucas," Camden & Atlantic Railroad, 1878; first engine with air brakes on Atlantic Division

245. No. 64, Northern Central Railroad, at Southport Yard, 1879.

46. The "Reuben Wells"—first locomotive to climb the Madison inclined plane without the use of cog-wheel and rack. It was placed in service in 1858, and remained in use regularly for 28 years, plus 10 years in partial service. The locomotive now preserved at Purdue University.

. No. 166, formerly the "Wheatland" of the Portage Railroad, as rebuilt in 1867. Originally built by Lancaster Locomotive Works in 1853. The small wheel behind the rear driver is part of the Loughridge Chain Brake system.

248. No. 90, Pittsburgh, Cincinnati & St. Louis, 1868.

249. No. 98, Philadelphia, Wilmington & Baltimore, built 1870.

250. No. 111, Northern Central Railroad, 1868.

251. No. 64, Philadelphia, Wilmington & Baltimore, in the '60's.

252. A Heavy Fast Passenger Engine of the Early '80's, Class K(D6). Drivers 78″ diam. Cylinders 18″ x 24″. Total weight 157,000 lb. Tractive force 11,860 lb.

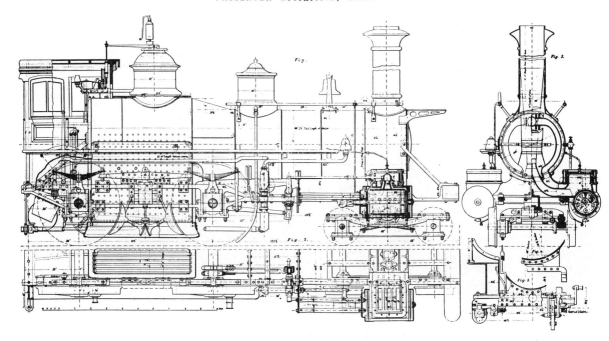

253. Class C, American Type. Many engines of this type were built at Altoona in the early '70's (reclassi-fied D3 and D4 anthracite). Drivers 62″ diam. Cylinders 17″ x 24″. Total weight 139,000 lb. Trac-tive force 11,890 lb.

TENDER FOR CLASS "C" ENGINES.

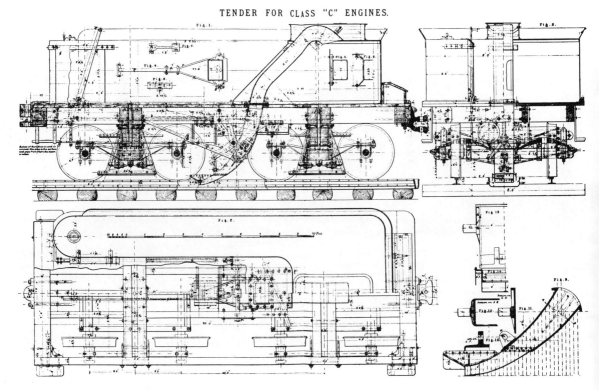

254. Tender for Class C engine.

255. First engines with Belpaire Fireboxes were the Class R(H3), built at Altoona in 1885 for freight service. Drivers 50″ diam. Cylinders 20″ x 24″. Total weight 190,000 lb. Tractive force 22,850 lb.

256. Classes O and P of the early '90's were excellent examples of passenger motive power, built at Altoona. Drivers 68″. Cylinders 18½″ x 24″. Total weight 192,000 lb. Tractive force 17,970 lb.

257. No. 14, West Jersey R.R., formerly Pennsylvania R.R. No. 55, Class D1.

258. The Class O(D10a), generally similar to Class P but lighter. Tractive force 15,550 lb.

259. Class F3c, the last of the Mogul Type freight locomotives, built 1901 to 1903. Drivers 62″ diam. Cylinders 20″ x 28″. Total weight 165,900 lb. Tractive force 31,480 lb.

260. No. 8542, tank engine, Lines West.

261. The Atlantic Type of 1902—an Altoona-built Class E3a. Drivers 80″ diam. Cylinders 22″ x 26″. Total weight 190,600 lb. Tractive force 27,410 lb.

262. An Atlantic built in 1908, Class E3sd at Germantown Junction (now North Philadelphia Station) in 1911. Specifications almost identical with No. 2773.

263. The first Class E6 Atlantic built 1910 at Altoona. Drivers 80″ diam. Cylinders 22″ x 26″. Total weigh 231,500 lb. Tractive force 27,410 lb.

64. Last of the Atlantic types is Class E6s. This engine is similar except that it had rotary valves—Class E6sa, 1910. Drivers 80″ diam. Cylinders 23½″ x 26″. Total weight 243,600 lb. Tractive force 31,275 lb.; with tender, 403,000 lb.

65. First Pennsylvania-designed Pacific type, the Class K2 of 1911. Drivers 80″. Cylinders 24″ x 26″. Total weight 278,800 lb.

266. Best-known of the Pacifics is the Class K4s. Here is the first of its kind, built at Altoona in 191[Drivers 80″. Cylinders 27″ x 28″. Total weight 308,890 lb. Tractive force 44,460 lb.; with tende 468,000 lb.

267. A K4s pulling the "American" in 1929.

268. First Pacific types with superheaters were these Baldwin built Class K3s of 1913. Drivers 80″ diam. Cylinders 26″ x 26″. Total weight 193,000 lb. Tractive force 38,280 lb.; with tender, 302,000 lb.

69. Class K21, an American Locomotive Company experimental Pacific.

0. A light 0-6-0 switcher of 1911, the Altoona-built Class B8. Drivers 56″ diam. Cylinders 20″ x 24″. Total weight 143,450 lb. Tractive force 29,870 lb.

271. Standard heavy six-wheel switcher is the Class B6sb built at Altoona through 1924. Drivers 56″ diam
Cylinders 22″ x 24″. Total weight 180,300 lb. Tractive force 36,140 lb.

272. Biggest articulated type ever used on the Pennsylvania—the Class HC1 built at Altoona in 191
Drivers 62″ diam. Cylinders (4) 30½″ x 32″. Total weight 603,500 lb. Tractive force 135,000 lb.; wi
tender 814,000 lb.

3. Latest design of Mountain type is the M1a built in 1930. Drivers 72″ diam. Cylinders 27″ x 30″. Total weight with tender 768,360 lb. Tractive force 64,550 lb.

74. Heaviest freight locomotive is the Decapod Class I1 first built in the early 1920's. Drivers 62″ diam. Cylinders 30½″ x 32″. Total weight with tender 590,000 lb. Tractive force 90,000 lb.

275. No. 3768, first of the streamlined Class K4s.

276. Four-cylindered Class T1, designed for fastest passenger service. Drivers 80″ diam. Cylinders 19¾ x 26″. Total weight with tender 930,200 lb. Tractive force 64,650 lb.

277. Four-cylindered freight locomotive Class Q1. Drivers 77″ diam. Cylinders, front 23″ x 28″; rear, 19½″ x 26″. Total weight with tender 1,027,870 lb. Tractive force 81,793 lb.; with booster 93,043 lb.

278. Four-cylindered freight locomotive Class Q2. Drivers 69″ diam. Cylinders, front 19¾″ x 28″; rear, 23¾″ x 29″. Total weight with tender 1,053,100 lb. Tractive force 99,860 lb.; with booster 114,860 lb

279. Class J1 freight locomotive of the 2-10-4 type. Drivers 69″ diam. Cylinders 29″ x 34″. Total weigh with tender 987,380 lb. Tractive force 95,100 lb.; with booster 110,100 lb.

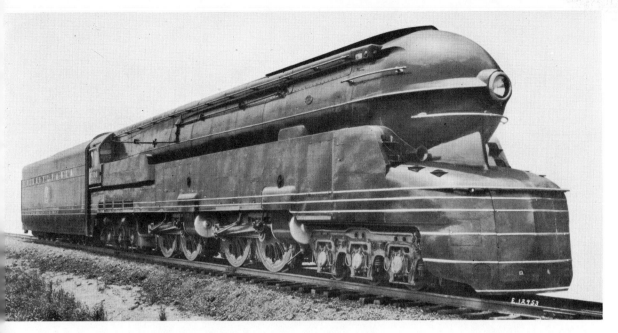

280. Largest and fastest steam passenger engine is the Class S1. Drivers 84″ diam. Cylinders 22″ x 26″. Total weight with tender 1,060,010 lb. Tractive force 71,900 lb.

81. First direct-drive steam turbine locomotive is the S2 Class. Drivers 68″ diam. No cylinders—direct-drive steam pressure 310 lb. Total weight with tender 1,032,100 lb. Tractive force 65,000 lb.

282. No. 3907, Class A6b, first Diesel engine.

283. No. 3909, Class AA6, 1,000 H.P. Diesel-electric switcher

284. A Baldwin Diesel passenger locomotive. It has four eight-cylinder 1,500-horsepower engines and 16 electric traction motors developing a tractive force of 204,500 lb. Total weight 1,187,420 lb.

285. New Electromotive Diesel Locomotive leaving Chicago with the Broadway Limited.

PART SIX

ELECTRIFICATION

THE FIRST lines of the Pennsylvania Railroad to be electrified were parts of the Long Island Railroad in 1905 and the West Jersey & Seashore Railroad from Camden to Atlantic City in 1906. These were planned for multiple-unit car operation, and this service on the Long Island has been extended to more than half the entire trackage. The power used was 600 volts D.C. supplied through a third rail, and when the Hudson and East River tunnels and Pennsylvania Station were planned the same system of current distribution was adopted. Today over a thousand multiple-unit cars are operated on the Long Island alone.

With the completion of the Hell Gate Bridge and a through route to New England, the New Haven's 11,000-volt single-phase A.C. system was extended to the Bowery Bay junction with the Long Island in 1918. Here interchange of Pennsylvania D.C. locomotives was made with New Haven A.C. engines on through passenger trains. In 1927 the freight line of the New York Connecting Railroad was similarly electrified, the operation of trains beginning in July. Thus through freight trains from Bay Ridge, after classification at Greenville yard, were thereafter electrically operated to Cedar Hill yard at New Haven.

While the work on the Hudson River tunnels and Pennsylvania Station was progressing, the type of electric locomotives to be used was an important consideration. Since few such engines had previously been built anywhere, several experimental locomotives were designed by railroad and Westinghouse engineers and tried on the West Jersey track (one is shown in illustration No. 290). From these tests a 4-4-0 type of locomotive was developed using 650 volts D.C., with side rods coupled to a jack shaft and from this, in turn, to a 2,000-horsepower motor mounted above the frame. Having a high center of gravity, it was not as destructive to the track as the gear-driven truck types. Classified as DD-1 and used in pairs back to back, 33 of these engines having Westinghouse equipment were built at Altoona. They were capable of the highest speeds yet attained by any electric locomotives. Since being placed in service in 1910, they have proved to be very efficient. Some are still in use on the Long Island Railroad.

A few years after the opening of Pennsylvania Station in New York, Philadelphia's Broad Street Station presented the next traffic problem which was to be solved by electrification. Here the increase in the number of passenger trains and especially a heavy suburban traffic required improvement of conditions, and in 1915 the 20 miles of main line to Paoli was electrified. In 1918 this was extended to the Chestnut Hill Branch and in 1924, the electrification of the Fort Washington Branch was completed. The line to Wilmington and the West Chester Branch were included in the program in 1928, and in 1930 Norristown had electric train service. The system originally decided upon in view of possible future main-line expansion was the 11,000-volt single-phase catenary type.

The first equipment to be put into service consisted of 93 motor cars (illustration No. 292), and by 1924 there were 286 cars of this type in use. By 1935 the motor and trailer equipment totaled 431 units; it now consists of 524 units. The most powerful single-unit electric locomotive ever built was tried in 1917 and used experimentally for a number of years. This was classed FF-1 and had a 2-8-8-2 wheel arrangement with side-rod drive, developing a tractive force of 140,000 pounds. In 1924 another type of side-rod locomotive was designed and three of these L5 engines were built. Two were D.C. engines for use in the New York electrified zone and the third, number 3930 (illustration No. 293), was A.C.-equipped and put in service at Philadelphia. Later 21 more L5 locomotives were built for the New York service. A six-wheeled switching engine was the next electric motive power designed, being classified as B-1. Of the first 16 A.C. engines, two were used at Philadelphia and 14 on the Bay Ridge line, while 12 D.C.-equipped engines were assigned to Sunnyside Yard.

Electrification of the Philadelphia–New York main line was carried on so that by 1930 service from Philadelphia to Trenton was started, and in January 1933 through main-line service between the principal cities was placed in operation. On January 28, 1935, the first test run of an electric train between Philadelphia and Washington occurred, and on the following February 10 the "Congressional Limited's" in both directions were the first trains in regular electric operation between New York and Washington, being drawn by the first of the GG-1 type locomotives. By March 15 all regular passenger trains between these cities were electrified, and shortly thereafter through trains to the west were electrically operated from New York to Paoli.

For the long-range electrification program, various types of locomotives were being designed. One was the O1 class, a light passenger type of the 4-4-4 wheel arrangement. Eight of these engines were built from June 1930 to December 1931. A 4-6-4 type classed as the P5 was also built, two being placed in service in July and August, 1931. Following these came the P5A, which was slightly heavier, also having a 4-6-4 wheel arrangement and being capable of 90 miles per hour speed, the tractive force being 56,250 pounds. In all, 89 of these locomotives were built; the first with box cabs were placed in service in 1932, and the following year the last 28 under construction were redesigned to have a streamline type of cab. Some of these engines were regeared for freight service.

In 1933, about the same time the P5A engines were undergoing the exterior changes, two entirely new locomotives were being planned, and these were completed in September 1934. One was the R-1, a 4-8-4 type, and the other was the first GG-1 class having a 4-6-0+0-6-4 wheel arrangement. The R-1 had a rigid frame for its four driving axles, while the GG-1 had two 4-6-0 frames which were articulated. Both these types, together with the O1, P5A, a New Haven Railroad 4-6-0+0-6-4 type electric, and a K4s steam locomotive, underwent exhaustive tests over a special section of test track near Claymont, Delaware. These tests, begun in 1933, were carried on for nearly two years.

As a result of these experiments, the GG-1 type was chosen and the construction of 57 locomotives was authorized, the first being completed in April and all by August 1935. With the use of these engines for passenger service, most of the P5A type were made available for freight service. When more GG-1s were built, some of these, too, were assigned to freight, there being a total of 139 engines of this type. Their continuous horsepower rating is 4,620 at speeds of 100 miles an hour.

To complete the electrification project initiated in 1928, work was started January 27, 1937, on the main line from Paoli to Harrisburg, the low-grade freight line from Morrisville through Columbia to Enola Yard, the freight line from Perryville to Columbia, and the freight line from Monmouth Junction to South Amboy. In less than a year—on the following January 15—the first passenger train, the Metropolitan, went into operation over the newly electrified line from Philadelphia to Harrisburg. On April 15 the electrified freight service from Harrisburg and Enola Yard east was inaugurated, thus completing the Pennsylvania's eastern seaboard electrification program. This makes a total of 2,677 miles of track now electrified, or 41 per cent of the total electrically operated standard railroad trackage of the United States.

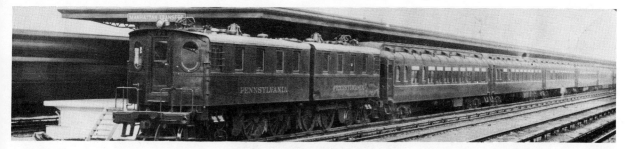

286a. Electrification into New York—a DD-1 locomotive and train at Manhattan Transfer, about 1920.

286b. Long Island Railroad electrification at Sunnyside.

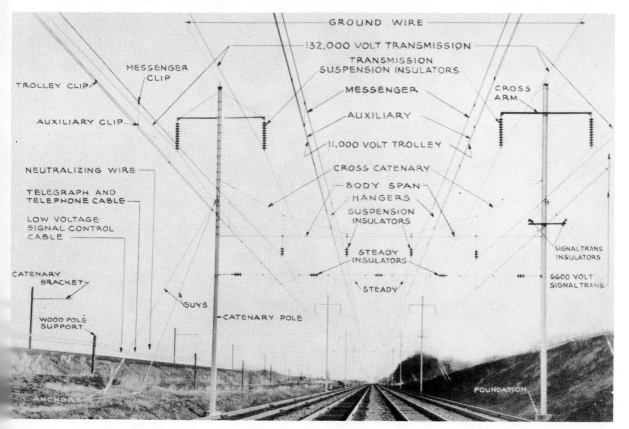

287. Typical catenary construction—names of component parts.

288. Wire trains—used in construction and service.

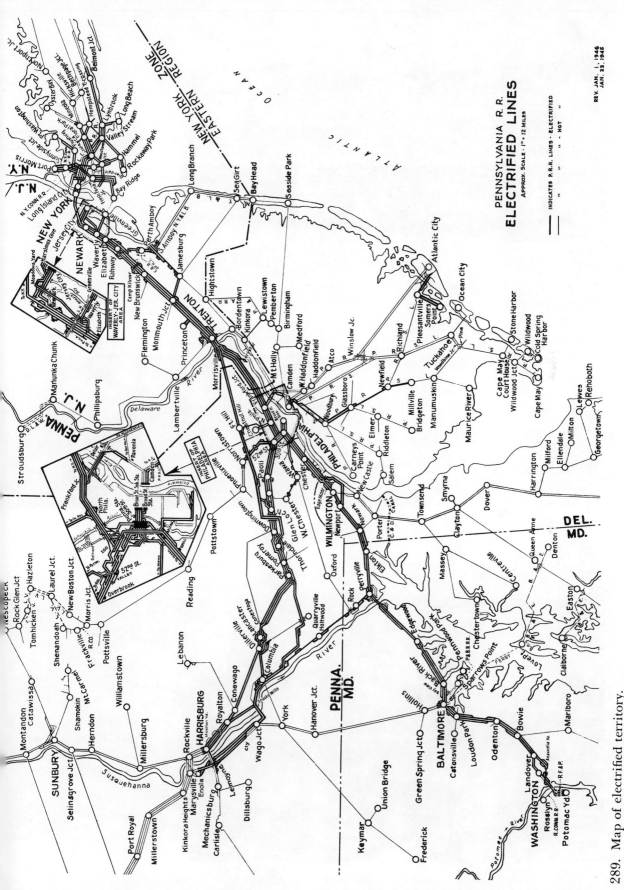

289. Map of electrified territory.

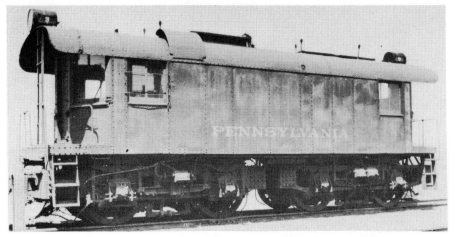

290. No. 9, first experimental electric locomotive, 1905.

291. No. 3931, the most powerful single-unit electric locomotive ever built, Class FF-1.

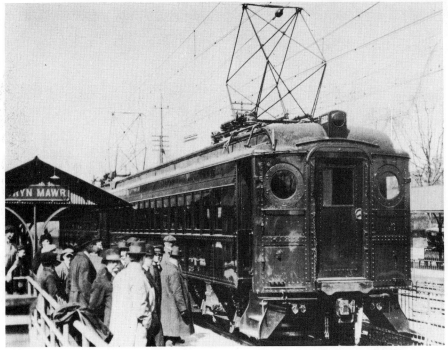

292. The first train of "M.U." cars on the Main Lines at Bryn Mawr, 1915.

293. No. 3930, Class L5 A.C. electric locomotive.

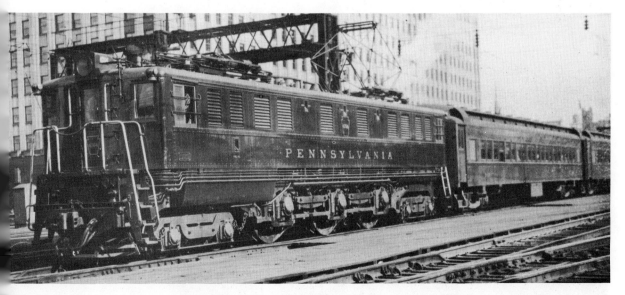

294. No. 4764, Class P5 locomotive.

295. First electric train to Harrisburg leaving Philadelphia January 15, 1938.

296. Interior of power director's room, Pennsylvania Station, New York.

297. Power dispatcher's room, Philadelphia.

298. Servicing a GG-1 locomotive.

99. No. 3900, a Class B2 switcher.

300. Electric locomotive for special service, at Cleveland dock.

301. Typical suburban station in electrified territory, Swarthmore, Pa.

PART SEVEN

SOME INCIDENTS OF

PENNSYLVANIA RAILROAD HISTORY

The Pittsburgh Riots of 1877

IN THE FIRST hundred years of the Pennsylvania Railroad's development, there have been many outstanding events. Besides the important circumstances of growth, operation, and improvement such as have already been mentioned, the railroad has weathered a number of disasters and unexpected incidents. The first of these might be the Civil War, during which it suffered some damage (Northern Central) but was of extreme importance in moving men and supplies, especially when the Baltimore & Ohio was partly in the hands of Confederate forces.

But far worse destruction of property came in 1877 as a result of riots in Pittsburgh. Their story begins with the depression following the panic of 1873 in which the railroads, largest business generally in the country, suffered most. A rate war on passenger and freight traffic resulted, and the only good feature of the situation was that the extremely low rates permitted large numbers of people to visit the Centennial Exposition in Philadelphia. According to Thomas A. Scott, then president of the Pennsylvania Railroad, "During the first six months of 1877, not a farthing was made on through competitive freight by any line." A new arrangement on rates among the eastern lines was made in April 1877, to take effect July 1, and a 10 per cent reduction of wages was ordered (a previous one had already been made in 1873). As a result, trouble was encountered on the Baltimore & Ohio at Martinsburg when firemen refused to accept the reduction ordered July 16 and, getting other employees to join them, soon blockaded the line. After this the strike quickly spread everywhere. Troops were called out, the President was called upon for aid, and Baltimore was the scene of considerable violence.

On the Pennsylvania the wage reduction order for all employees and officers had gone into effect on June 1 and had been accepted—though, of course, not too cheerfully. What precipitated the trouble was another order effective July 19 for double-heading all freight trains between Pittsburgh and Altoona instead of operating trains in two sections. Although some trains had already gone out as doubleheaders on the morning of the 19th, the two brakemen and the flagman of the 8:40 from Pittsburgh refused to leave. When the dispatcher recruited a crew from yardmen, the strikers attacked them with coupling pins and would not permit any trains to leave the yard, persuading all the incoming freight crews to join them. Thus began one of the worst strikes and riots in the United States.

Soon the railroad property was in the strikers' hands; though passenger trains were allowed to run, freight traffic was halted. No help was forthcoming from the Mayor or police, and by late evening the acting superintendent at Pittsburgh asked protection from the sheriff, who tried to reason with the crowd. Failing in this, he wired the governor for aid. The governor was traveling outside of the state at the time, but the adjutant-general ordered General Pearson with three regiments to the scene, one of which, the 18th, was sent to the stockyards. The members of the other two sympathized with the strike and fraternized with the crowd, only about 230 having been assembled by the evening of the 20th. Meanwhile the First Division of the National Guard had been ordered to Pittsburgh.

On the morning of the 21st the militia were ordered to hold the 28th Street crossing, a mile east of the Union Station, and by 3 P.M. the National Guard troops, mostly men from Philadelphia, arrived at Union Station. Since it was Saturday, a half holiday, the crowd now consisted largely of mill and factory hands and miners who had heard about the trouble at Baltimore. Many hoodlums, tramps, and rowdies swelled the mob, and most of the destruction that followed is attributed to this element. When the troops left the station for 28th Street, they were given instructions that not a shot was to be fired, but otherwise to defend themselves if necessary. Upon reaching the crossing, they found the Pittsburgh militia fraternizing with a mob of thousands. When the troops attempted to clear the tracks, the rioters pressed them, throwing coal and firing pistols. Eventually, after some of the mob tried to take the soldiers' muskets, firing began. It lasted only about a minute, but at least sixteen of the mob were killed and a number wounded, and the mob dispersed temporarily.

At dark the troops were taken to the lower roundhouse at 26th Street for food and rest, and the Pittsburgh militia were supposed to occupy the upper roundhouse at 28th Street. The food never arrived, the wagons being intercepted by the crowd. However, so many militiamen had deserted and were friendly to the mob that the remaining few were dismissed, leaving only the Philadelphia troops, who, incidentally, had had very little food since starting their journey. Meanwhile the rioters again assembled, many having broken into gunshops for weapons, and a number of volleys were aimed at the roundhouse windows. Two or three of the mob were killed after being warned when they tried to use a field piece. The rioters then tried to fire the roundhouse, but for a while the troops kept the fires under control with fire apparatus. The report of the Pennsylvania Legislative Committee appointed to investigate the riots says:

> Tired, hungry, worn out, surrounded by a mob of infuriated men yelling like demons, fire on nearly all sides of them, suffocated and blinded by smoke, with no chance to rest and little knowledge of what efforts were being made for their relief, with orders not to fire on the mob unless in necessary self-defense, the wonder is that they were not totally demoralized; but the evidence of all the officers is that the men behaved like veterans.

By now the mob had set fire to the other railroad buildings in the yard and to the rolling stock. Whiskey from pillaged freights added to the mob's frenzy, and still more cars were plundered. Eventually the round-house caught fire, and about 8 A.M. Sunday the 22nd, the troops marched out. Although the mob made way, they were fired on from the rear. Refused admittance to the United States Arsenal, they crossed the Allegheny River, camped, and were soon fed through the efforts of Pennsylvania Railroad officials—the first food they had had in more than 24 hours. Three or four had been killed and 13 wounded. As for the rioters, although coroner's inquests were held over 19 bodies, more were believed to have been otherwise disposed of.

That Sunday the destruction and plundering went on, and in the afternoon the Union Station and Hotel and the grain elevator were burned. By then the mob was too drunk to do more damage, and the riot was over. Besides the buildings mentioned, all the shops, engine houses, offices and depots—some 39 buildings—had been destroyed. The rolling stock burned totaled 46 passenger cars and 506 freight cars, and those of the lines west of Pittsburgh came to 20 passenger cars and 861 freight cars. Also destroyed were 104 locomotives and, of course, the contents of the freight cars—the entire loss being placed at over $5,000,000. Eventually, by July 29, the first freight train moved out and the strike was over, the men returning to work without having the former rate of pay restored. Other cities were also affected, such as Chicago, where 10 rioters were killed, but the trouble generally was ended by July 31. It is interesting to note that while these events were taking place, the mail trains were not interfered with and through passenger trains also ran, mostly over the Conemaugh division. The Pennsylvania Railroad and the various shippers and others who had large property damage brought suit against Allegheny County for the losses, and in 1879 the railroad's claims were settled for $1,600,000.

The Johnstown Flood

In 1889 the Johnstown Flood caused considerable damage to the Pennsylvania Railroad besides the havoc brought to the many communities along the Conemaugh River and undetermined loss of life, estimated to be well over 3,000. So many detailed accounts, such as "The Johnstown Horror" and "The Story of Johnstown," have appeared that only a few particulars of its effect upon the railroad are pertinent here.

The story originates in 1836, when a reservoir to supply a water deficiency in the Western Division Canal was authorized by the State Legislature. This was located ten miles east of Johnstown, on South Fork Creek two miles above its junction with the Conemaugh River. Begun in 1838, it was not completed until 1853. It then formed the largest artificial lake in the country. When the Pennsylvania Railroad purchased the State System in 1857, it was abandoned and after passing through various hands was finally sold in May 1879 to the South Fork Fishing and Hunting Club. The dam was restored and heightened, and after 1881 the lake it formed was known as Lake Conemaugh, the club restricting its use exclusively to its own members. The dam was evidently not properly maintained, and two years before the disaster, when a sudden flood inundated the Conemaugh Valley, it was feared that the dam might go.

In the latter part of May 1889 an unprecedented rainfall for central and western Pennsylvania began and continued for several days until the Conemaugh River had covered parts of Johnstown to a depth of three feet. South Fork Creek became a torrent which, flowing into Lake Conemaugh, raised the level of the lake until water started pouring over the dam. Warning messages were sent to the towns along the valley below, but they were ignored. Just before 3 P.M. the center of the dam gave way and the worst flood in the country's history began.

The Pennsylvania Railroad was considerably damaged: over ten miles of track were entirely destroyed, so completely that at various places the original location of the track was hard to determine. Several large bridges, the stone Conemaugh viaduct, the roundhouse, machine shops, and the yard at Conemaugh were entirely washed away. Some 34 locomotives, 24 passenger cars, and 561 freight cars were also lost and damaged, and so powerful was the wall of water that some locomotives were carried more than a mile downstream.

Conemaugh, about a mile and a half above Johnstown, was the scene of a railroad thriller far more exciting than most fiction. Although most of those involved were saved, about 26 people lost their lives in attempting to escape from the two sections of No. 8, the Day Express. The story as published a few months later follows.

The two sections composing this train eastward left Pittsburgh at the usual hour on Friday morning, with a liberal complement of passengers. The swollen Conemaugh, whose banks the main line of the Pennsylvania Railroad follows for forty miles, looked threatening as it bore off numberless saw-logs and masses of drift-wood. At Johnstown the streets were submerged and reports of landslides and washouts caused a delay. Proceeding to East Conemaugh, the sections were run on separate tracks, with a freight train between them. Other freights occupied different positions near the depot and the mail train was placed in the rear of the first section of the express. Telegraph wires and poles had fallen and definite information regarding the track could not be obtained by the anxious railway officials. For a time the passengers sought to dispel their uneasiness by reading and chatting. Three weary hours passed. Whispers that the dam at Lake Conemaugh might break blanched the faces of the stoutest. Assistant-Superintendent Tromp had gone a couple of miles farther, with an engine and coach, to ascertain the state of affairs. Another locomotive, handled by Engineer John Hess, was stationed a mile east of the express train as a precaution. Rain beat on the cars and the wind moaned distressfully. Each moment seemed a short eternity, nor could the feeling of impending evil be shaken off. Most of the passengers on the mail train were familiar with the country and knew the dangerous situation, should the reservoir burst its bounds. They left the train about noon, but the through passengers stayed in the vestibuled parlor cars of the Day Express. At last the shrieks of a locomotive whistle were heard, sounding like the wailings of a lost soul. The passengers rose from their seats instinctively, realizing that something serious had happened. A conductor or brakeman entered each coach and remarked quietly:

"Please step up on the hill-side as quickly as possible!"

There was no time for explanation and none was needed. No time for lingering farewell, last kiss and fond caress. Already the roar of advancing waters filled the air. Those who first reached the platform saw wrecked houses, broken bridges, trees and rocks borne on a tidal wave just turning the bend three hundred yards away. Frantic exertions were made to escape to the protecting hills back of the station. An old mill-race, never filled up, was in the way, with narrow planks for crossings. Some of the terrified passengers jumped or fell into the waters and drowned, the deluge from the reservoir overtaking them as they floundered in the ditch. A few of those who could not leave the train survived with painful bruises, a drenching and a paralyzing fright, the waters rising half-way to the car-roofs. Several were caught in the deadly swirl as they tried to crawl under the vestibuled coaches of the second section, which lay on the inside track. It was the work of a moment to envelop the trains. The horror-stricken spectators beheld a sight unexampled in the history of railroading. An ominous roar and the round-house and nine heavy engines disappeared. Everything in the line of the flood was displaced or swallowed up. Locomotives were tossed aside and their tenders spirited off. A baggagecar of the mail train broke its couplings and drifted out of view, while the rear car swung around at right angles to the track. A pullman coach rolled off and was crushed, a resident picking up one of its gas fixtures next day at the lower end of Woodvale. Mere playthings for the whirlpool, engines and cars were hidden beneath timbers, brush and dirt. Slaked by the water, a cargo of lime on the train between the sections of the express set two Pullman coaches blazing. Thus fire and flood combined to lend fresh horrors to the onslaught. The coaches burned to the trucks. By five o'clock the force of the torrent had subsided and an estimate of the carnage was attempted. Hardly a shred was saved from the trains, the passengers having left baggage and garments in their frenzied flight. Many had neither hats nor wraps but this was scarcely thought of in the confusion and excitement. Bitter lamentations for missing ones tempered the joy of the survivors over their own safety.

Upon the first warning of the death-dealing wave Engineer Hess tied the whistle of his locomotive open, put on all steam and dashed towards East Conemaugh. The whistle screamed and howled as if a tortured fiend possessed it, bringing people to their doors in hot haste and enabling hundreds to flee to high ground ere their houses were engulfed. The brave engineer jumped from the iron steed barely in time to save his life by a hasty race beyond the invading waters. Next instant the flood swept the engine from the track, whirling and rolling it over and over, and embedded it in the dirt. Lying bruised and pummelled and disabled, pitiful was its helplessness compared with its strength as it had stood upon the track in its burnished bravery of steel and brass, ready at the lever's touch to pluck big handfuls of power and fling them in fleecy volumes to the skies. Silent was the whistle that had informed the passengers and citizens of the coming destruction. During the height of the flood the sound of locomotive whistles from the midst of the waters startled and surprised the fugitives huddled on the hill. Two engineers, with the nerve typical of their class, had stuck to their cabs. While awful wreck and devastation environed them, the brazen throats pealed a defiant note at intervals, the last time with exultant vigor as the waters were slowly receding. Locomotive 1309, a fifty-ton eight-wheeler, stood in its place, smoke curling from its stack, steam issuing from the safety-valve, and driftwood heaped up to the top of the headlight, the glass in which, by a queer fantasy of the flood, was not cracked. Not far away Locomotive 477, its tender tipped over, a mass of refuse surrounding it, headed the train which sustained the least damage. The mighty arms were powerless and the fiery bosom was chilled. Engineer Henry, who escaped to the hills, could not restrain a sigh at the sight of his giant pet, feeble and useless in the midst of a waste that so much needed the assistance of the strong to bring order out of chaos.

Ohio Floods

More disastrous floods occurred in 1913, this time in the valley of the Ohio River and its tributaries—the Muskingum, Scioto and Miami rivers. A serious windstorm on March 21 was the prelude to several days of continued downpour, the average for Ohio being over 7 inches in that time. All the streams and rivers overflowed, submerging hundreds of towns and cities, destroying bridges and roadbeds and causing a loss of life estimated to be over 500. Dayton was particularly hard hit, and the cities of Hamilton, Columbus, Zanesville, Cincinnati, and Piqua were entirely or partly under water. Hundreds of millions of dollars' damage was done, and of the railroads, the Pennsylvania and its affiliates—Vandalia and the Pittsburgh, Cincinnati, Chicago & St. Louis—were the most damaged, their cost of reconstruction alone totaling $3,500,000.

Again through the 17th to the 20th of March, 1936, extremely heavy rainfall caused destructive floods in most of Pennsylvania, especially the western portion on both sides of the Appalachian divide. The waters of all rivers and tributaries rose to heights of five or six feet more than any previous recordings, this being occasioned by the combination of the torrential rains and the run-off from melting snow and ice. Considerable undermining and washing out of roadbed, along the Juniata, Conemaugh, and Susquehanna rivers interrupted main-line traffic for three and a half days. To restore service, an army of 15,000 men and 150 work trains was busy as soon as the waters had receded sufficiently to allow removal of debris and the making of necessary track repairs.

Once more, early in the following year, a devastating flood affected the Pennsylvania and, of course, all other railroads in the Ohio valley. Termed the Ohio River's worst flood, it followed a series of storms over the Ohio River basin, the first of which lasted from January 7 to January 10. The second began on the 13th and continued until the 19th. This left most of the Ohio's tributaries well above flood stage. The third commenced after only a day's interruption and ended on the 25th. The result was not only the highest water level ever recorded, 80 feet at Cincinnati, but a longer-lasting flood than any previous one. Even the new Union Terminal at Cincinnati was out of service by noon of the 22nd and was not reopened for passenger traffic until February 4. Not quite as much damage was done to tracks or bridges as in the previous flood, but traffic was suspended generally until February 8 in the Cincinnati area.

Broad Street Station Fire

Shortly after midnight on the morning of June 11, 1923, fire was discovered under one of the platforms of Broad Street Station. Spreading swiftly, the flames soon reached the train shed, and practically all of Philadelphia's fire department with nearly every piece of apparatus was called to the scene. Although brought under control by noon, it was two more days before the fire was entirely out, with the structure left in ruins.

Almost as spectacular as the blaze itself were the preparations and work done to maintain traffic as nearly normal as possible. Even before the fire was at its height, plans were made to receive incoming trains and dispatch outgoing ones at other Pennsylvania stations in the city. At the time, Broad Street Station handled the heaviest passenger traffic on the system—some 530 trains which required 2,217 engine and train movements in and out being scheduled every 24 hours. A large proportion of the commuters of the city helped bring the total number of passengers using the station to nearly 80,000 daily, and to avoid delaying this traffic was the goal aimed at and attained. In fact, every one of the arriving trains was taken care of and 95 per cent of those outbound were dispatched as planned. The following day all trains were operated, and at no time were through trains or sleeping cars canceled.

Before morning, while the fire was still burning, temporary construction of platforms and stairways to the street was begun. These were some distance beyond the end of the train shed and away from the heat and flames. On the day of the fire 38 suburban trains used this platform, and on the following day 142 operated to and from it. Five days after the fire was out all 16 tracks had been rebuilt with adjoining platforms and 70 per cent of the former service had been restored. The rest of the trains were handled from West Philadelphia because of using 6 of the tracks for equipment needed for dismantling the train shed.

Before the fire was entirely out and as the warped girders of the track supports and roof arches cooled, the rebuilding of the track and platforms was started. By Wednesday, June 13, the first platform from the train gates to the outer end of the train shed was finished. This allowed passengers to use the station directly again instead of by means of the temporary stairways. On the same day full electric suburban service, consisting of 151 trains, was restored and on the following day two tracks were completed all the way to the train gates.

The Pennsylvania Railroad versus Snow

Snow has never been quite as great a handicap to the Pennsylvania Railroad as it has been to western and northern railroads. There have been times, however, when it has caused serious trouble, and the railroad is always prepared for any such eventuality. One of the worst tie-ups in the last half century was caused by the Blizzard of March 1914, which crippled all railroads in New Jersey more than any other storm in their history. So severe was the blizzard that many trains were snowed in and no train left Philadelphia or New York for 24 hours. About 1,600 miles of track were affected, and most of the 6,855 miles of telegraph and telephone wires were brought down by the heavy snow and ice.

The storm began with snow and rain on Sunday morning, March 1, and by early afternoon the temperature dropped below the freezing point. Many early reports of trouble reached the headquarters of the New York Division at Jersey City, but these suddenly stopped and all communication between New York and Philadelphia and towns in between ended by 6 P.M., indicating that all wires were down. By 7:30 no more trains left New York or Jersey City, and the last train from Philadelphia left at midnight—about which time the worst part of the storm arrived. The Broadway Limited left New York at 2:45 Sunday afternoon and reached North Philadelphia at 1 o'clock the next morning. The next four trains following within the hour managed to reach Philadelphia about seven hours late, but the thirteen trains after these were snow-bound at various points along the New York Division.

Actually, the Division was tied up as much by fallen poles and wires as by the snow and drifts. With no communication the task of clearing the line was made much more difficult. The Chief Dispatcher, the train-master, and other officers left their offices and personally directed operations when no reports were available. Over 2,300 regular employees and 5,000 extra laborers and all work train equipment possible were enlisted to restore service. Some eastbound trains managed to reach Manhattan Transfer and New York after being stranded for hours, but at 9 o'clock on Monday morning westbound trains were still stalled. At that time there were 18 trains with 2,000 passengers marooned between New York and Philadelphia. Water ran low on some engines and the fires had to be put out; work trains helped push these trains to stations and supplied steam for keeping the passenger cars warm. Tender tanks of others at New Brunswick were filled by the fire department's hoses. Few signals were operating, and orders for all movements of trains were issued verbally by train dispatchers until wires were replaced.

Special commissary trains were run to feed the army of laborers. Many of the stalled trains had dining cars, so the passengers were fed, meals being free; others had meals brought to them by an extra engine at New Brunswick. Passengers of two trains which reached Trenton by noon Monday were sent to hotels there as guests of the Pennsylvania, later proceeding when the trains could move. The "Congressional Limited," also stalled all night, kept its diner open and with sufficient steam from the engine the cars were kept comfortable.

When it was evident that the blizzard had really brought traffic to a standstill, the following notice was posted at Pennsylvania Station:

> The road is tied up as far west as Trenton, and there is no possibility that trains will move today. Trains may move this evening, and full announcements will be made well in advance of each departure. Persons having New York hotel or residence addresses are advised to leave their telephone numbers with the station master and return to their homes to wait the departure of trains in comfort.

Pullman cars in the station accommodated 800 people that Sunday night, 2,500 people in all sleeping either in trains or in waiting rooms.

By Monday night, all the delayed trains were on their way, and at 8 A.M. on Tuesday regular trains started operating. By Wednesday, trains were leaving New York and Philadelphia on time but arriving one to two hours late. This delay was caused by the necessity for running slowly, as dispatchers had considerable difficulty in getting orders to the trains. Wednesday's operation improved, and by that evening trains were on time—quite an accomplishment considering the lack of telegraph wires.

302. Callowhill Street Bridge during the Centennial Exposition, 1876, with Pennsylvania tracks below.

303. A special excursion train for the Centennial.

304. During the Railroad Riots of 1877 the Pittsburgh installations suffered severe damage, as seen in these photographs of the ruins of the main passenger depot, the roundhouse, and the trackside.

305. A general view of the aftermath of the Johnstown flood, 1889.

306. The Day Express was caught by the Johnstown flood.

307. Wreckage of a Class R engine caught by the flood.

308. The temporary trestle replacing the Conemaugh viaduct destroyed by the Johnstown flood.

309. Bridge number 145 wrecked by the Ohio flood of March 1913.

310. Freight yard at Zanesville after the Ohio flood of 1913.

A

B

C

D

311. The Broad Street Station fire, 1923. A. General view of the train shed, B. Looking west from station building, C. Filbert Street side during the fire, D. A K4s engine and cars damaged by fire.

312. Snow blocks.

E P I L O G U E

AT THE END of its first century, the Pennsylvania Railroad was owned by about 218,000 stockholders, and through all these years dividends have been paid continuously since 1847—an unequaled record. A capital investment of over three billion dollars is represented in its facilities and resources. Its gross revenues are greater than those of any other railroad in the United States, and it carries the greatest freight tonnage among all systems. It is the country's largest coal carrier, more than 21 per cent of the total freight revenue coming from this source—47 per cent of all the soft coal and 53 per cent of all the anthracite mined being transported over its lines. Freight receipts account for 67 per cent of the gross revenues, and passenger receipts are 25.8 per cent.

The Pennsylvania is the fourth largest system in point of mileage operated, there being some 10,683 miles of main and branch lines. About half the country's population lives in territory reached by Pennsylvania lines in 14 states and the District of Columbia, in which two-thirds of the total wealth and resources of the nation are also concentrated.

Besides its own lines, the Pennsylvania has substantial investments in several other roads. These include almost a half ownership of the Norfolk & Western, a full ownership of the Long Island, a one-sixth interest in the Richmond, Fredericksburg and Potomac, a half ownership of the New York Connecting Railroad, a 30 per cent interest in the Lehigh Valley, and a large percentage of the voting interest in the Wabash.

MOTIVE POWER ON THE PENNSYLVANIA RAILROAD AS OF JULY 1, 1947, INCLUDING LONG ISLAND RAILROAD

STEAM

CLASS	UNITS	CLASS	UNITS	CLASS	UNITS	CLASS	UNITS
A5s	46	H8sb	22	L1s (of)	9	E6s (of)	1
B6	9	H8sc	54	L2s	5	G5s	121
B6s	69	H9s	538	M1	201	K2s	7
B6sa	50	H9sa	13	M1a	84	K2sa	7
B6sb	233	H9sc	9	M1b	16	K3s	12
B8	44	H10s (hf)	369	N1s	60	K4s	417
B8a	20	H10s (s)	45	N2sa	130	K4sa	5
B28s	30	I1s	109	Q1	1	K5	2
C1	90	I1sa	489	Q2	26	S1	1
C51s	4						
C51sa	15						
CC25	10	J1	65	D16sb	3	S2	1
G53sd	6						
HH1	6	J1a	60	E3sd	5	T1	52
H6sb	117	L1s (s)	513	E5s	7		
H8sa	27	L1s (hf)	39	E6s (hf)	73		

ELECTRIC

CLASS	UNITS	CLASS	UNITS	CLASS	UNITS	CLASS	UNITS
A1	2						
B1	28	O1	2	*A6b	1	*AA2	1
B3	14						
DD1	23						
DD2	1	O1a	2	*AS-6	8	*AA3	1
GG1	139	O1b	2	*BS-6	13		
L6	2	O1c	2	*ES-6	10		
L6a	1	R1	1	*BS-10	8		
P5	2	DD1	8	*ES-10	3		
P5a	89	Odd	2	*BP-1	3		
P56	1	†A6	2	*EP-3	1		

* oil electric
† gas electric

SUMMARY

	STEAM	ELECTRIC	TOTAL
Shifting	610	91	701
Freight	3023	140	3163
Passenger	714	141	855
Total	4347	372	4719

I N D E X